lonely planet

BEST ROAD TRIPS

MIDWEST & THE GREAT LAKES

– – – – – – – – →

ESCAPES ON THE OPEN ROAD

T0016990

Mark Baker, Ryan ver Berkmoes,
Ali Lemer, Karla Zimmerman

HOW TO USE THIS BOOK

Reviews

In the Destinations section:

All reviews are ordered in our authors' preference, starting with their most preferred option. Additionally:

Sights are arranged in the geographic order that we suggest you visit them and, within this order, by author preference.

Eating and Sleeping reviews are ordered by price range (budget, midrange, top end) and, within these ranges, by author preference.

Map Legend

Routes

- Trip Route
- Trip Detour
- Linked Trip
- Walk Route
- Tollway
- Freeway
- Primary
- Secondary
- Tertiary
- Lane
- Unsealed Road
- Plaza/Mall
- Steps
-)=(Tunnel
- Pedestrian Overpass
- Walk Track/Path

Boundaries

- International
- State/Province
- Cliff

Hydrography

- River/Creek
- Intermittent River
- Swamp/Mangrove
- Canal
- Water
- Dry/Salt/ Intermittent Lake
- Glacier

Route Markers

- 97 US National Hwy
- 5 US Interstate Hwy
- 44 State Hwy

Trips

- 1 Trip Numbers
- 9 Trip Stop
- Walking tour
- Trip Detour

Population

- ✪ Capital (National)
- ◉ Capital (State/Province)
- ● City/Large Town
- ○ Town/Village

Areas

- Beach
- Cemetery (Christian)
- Cemetery (Other)
- Park
- Forest
- Reservation
- Urban Area
- Sportsground

Transport

- ✈ Airport
- Ⓑ BART station
- Ⓣ Boston T station
- ⌖ Cable Car/ Funicular
- Ⓜ Metro/Muni station
- Ⓟ Parking
- Ⓢ Subway station
- ⌖ Train/Railway
- ⌖ Tram
- Ⓤ Underground station

Note: Not all symbols displayed above appear on the maps in this book

Symbols In This Book

✓ Top Tips	🍷 Food & Drink
🔗 Link Your Trips	🌳 Outdoors
Tips from Locals	📷 Essential Photo
🚗 Trip Detour	🚶 Walking Tour
📖 History & Culture	🍴 Eating
👪 Family	🛏 Sleeping

◉ Sights		🛏 Sleeping
🏖 Beaches		🍴 Eating
🏃 Activities		🍷 Drinking
🎓 Courses		☆ Entertainment
☞ Tours		🔒 Shopping
🎉 Festivals & Events		ⓘ Information & Transport

These symbols and abbreviations give vital information for each listing:

📞 Telephone number		🐾 Pet-friendly
☉ Opening hours		🚌 Bus
🅿 Parking		⛴ Ferry
⊘ Nonsmoking		🚊 Tram
❄ Air-conditioning		🚆 Train
@ Internet access		apt apartments
📶 Wi-fi access		d double rooms
🏊 Swimming pool		dm dorm beds
🍴 Vegetarian selection		q quad rooms
📖 English-language menu		r rooms
		s single rooms
👪 Family-friendly		ste suites
		tr triple rooms
		tw twin rooms

CONTENTS

PLAN YOUR TRIP

ROAD TRIPS

DESTINATIONS

COVID-19

We have re-checked every business in this book before publication to ensure that it is still open after the COVID-19 outbreak. However, the economic and social impacts of COVID-19 will continue to be felt long after the outbreak has been contained, and many businesses, services and events referenced in this guide may experience ongoing restrictions. Some businesses may be temporarily closed, have changed their opening hours and services, or require bookings; some unfortunately could have closed their doors permanently. We suggest you check with venues before visiting for the latest information.

Sleeping Bear Dunes National Lakeshore (p97) Storm clouds over Lake Michigan

WELCOME TO
MIDWEST & THE GREAT LAKES

Don't be fooled by all the corn. The Midwest is much more than a flat, endless field. Intrepid road-trippers will find that out as soon as they set wheels on red-cliffed Hwy 61 in northern Minnesota. Or on the dune-backed thoroughfares of western Michigan.

The Great Lakes are huge, like inland seas. Dairy farms and orchards blanket the region, meaning fresh pie and ice cream await trip-takers. Roll call for the region's cities starts with Chicago, which unfurls what is arguably the country's mightiest skyline.

Many sights lie near the interstates that span these beguiling wide-open spaces, but many more are found along the ever-intriguing small roads – the 'blue highways' of lore.

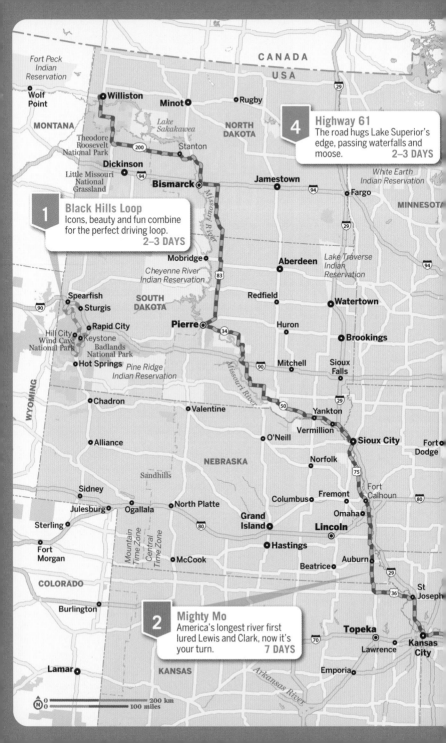

CANADA

USA

Fort Peck Indian Reservation

● Wolf Point

● **Williston**

● **Minot**

● Rugby

MONTANA

NORTH DAKOTA

Lake Sakakawea

4 Highway 61
The road hugs Lake Superior's edge, passing waterfalls and moose. **2–3 DAYS**

Theodore Roosevelt National Park

Stanton

Dickinson ●

White Earth Indian Reservation

Little Missouri National Grassland

Bismarck ●

Jamestown ●

● Fargo

MINNESOTA

Missouri River

1 Black Hills Loop
Icons, beauty and fun combine for the perfect driving loop. **2–3 DAYS**

Mobridge ●

Cheyenne River Indian Reservation

Aberdeen ●

Lake Traverse Indian Reservation

Spearfish ●
● Sturgis

SOUTH DAKOTA

Redfield ●

Watertown ●

Rapid City ●

Hill City ● ● Keystone
Wind Cave National Park

Badlands National Park

Pierre ◉

Huron ●

Brookings ●

● Hot Springs

Pine Ridge Indian Reservation

Mitchell ●

Sioux Falls ●

WYOMING

● Chadron

● Valentine

Missouri River

Yankton ●

Vermillion ●

Sioux City ●

Fort ● Dodge

● Alliance

O'Neill ●

NEBRASKA

Norfolk ●

Sandhills

Sidney ●

Julesburg ●

Ogallala ●

● North Platte

Columbus ●

Fremont ●

Fort Calhoun

Sterling ●

Mountain Time Zone | *Central Time Zone*

Grand Island ●

Omaha ●

Lincoln ◉

Fort Morgan ●

● McCook

● Hastings

Auburn ●

COLORADO

Beatrice ●

St Joseph

Burlington ●

2 Mighty Mo
America's longest river first lured Lewis and Clark, now it's your turn. **7 DAYS**

Topeka ◉

Kansas City

Lamar ●

KANSAS

Lawrence ●

Arkansas River

Emporia ●

Ⓝ 0 ___ 200 km
0 ___ 100 miles

MIDWEST & THE GREAT LAKES

★

3 **Michigan's Gold Coast**
Lake Michigan's shore features beaches, wineries and island-hopping. **4 DAYS**

ort rances

Grand Portage

Grand Marais

Tofte

Isle Royale National Park

Lake Superior

61

Two Harbors

Apostle Islands

Duluth • Knife River

wa al t

Ottawa National Forest

Rock River Canyon Wilderness

Escanaba

Mackinaw City

119

Lake Huron

35

Petoskey

Leland

31

75

Huron National Forest

West Branch

St Paul
opolis

Eau Claire

39

Menominee

22

Traverse City

27

35

Green Bay

Manistee

Saginaw Bay

MICHIGAN

Appleton

Manitowoc

31

Manistee National Forest

75

Fond Du Lac

WISCONSIN

43

Muskegon

Grand Rapids

Lansing

Madison

Milwaukee

94

Lake Michigan

Holland

Janesville

Saugatuck • Fennville

Marshall

Jackson

IOWA

Dubuque

Rockford

94

69

23

Waterloo

Three Oaks

Buchanan

Cedar Rapids

Iowa City/ Coralville

Chicago

New Buffalo

Elkhart

es Moines

Davenport

Joliet

Gary

80

Fort Wayne

57

Galesburg

65

INDIANA

69

OHIO

Burlington

Peoria

Bloomington

Lafayette

ILLINOIS

55

Danville

MISSOURI

Quincy

Champaign

Indianapolis

72

Springfield

Terre Haute

Columbus

Arrow Rock

Columbia

St Charles

57

70

Scottsburg

Jefferson City

St Louis

Vincennes

Frankfort

64

Louisville

Mark Twain National Forest

44

55

Evansville

Ohio River

KENTUCKY

Mississippi River

Des Moines River

Missouri River

ARTIST: CHUCK BERRY BY HARRY WEBER; IMAGE: JAMES KIRKIKIS/SHUTTERSTOCK ©

St Louis (left) Immerse yourself in the blues rhythms of one of America's great old cities. See it on Trip 2

Michigan's Western Shore (above) Beach lounging, dune climbing, berry eating and surfing. See it on Trip 3

Kansas City (right) Nothing beats eating yourself silly on amazing barbecue while grooving to Kansas City jazz. See it on Trip 2

Chicago River Skyscrapers in the downtown area

CHICAGO

Take cloud-scraping architecture, lakefront beaches and world-class museums, stir in wild comedy, divey blues clubs and hefty pizzas, and you've got a town that won't let you down. The city center is a steely wonder, but it's the mural-splashed neighborhoods where Chicago's true heart beats.

Getting Around

Driving Chicago's well laid-out street grid is slow, but not too difficult, except around the Loop. If you're exploring downtown and other neighborhoods served by public transportation, ditch your car for the day and get around on foot and by L train instead.

Parking

Overnight hotel parking and city parking garages are expensive. Metered on-street parking is easier to find in outlying neighborhoods than around downtown; look for a pay box on the block. Some meter-free neighborhoods require resident parking passes, some don't. Read signs carefully.

Where to Eat

Essential eats include Chicago-style hot dogs, Italian beef sandwiches and deep-dish pizza. Star chefs run restaurants in the West Loop and on the Near North Side. For an eclectic mix of cafes, bistros, gastropubs and more, nose around Wicker Park, Pilsen, Logan Square and Andersonville.

Where to Stay

The Loop and Near North feature cool design hotels and chain properties convenient for sightseeing and transportation. The West Loop flaunts the trendiest quarters. Posh hostels and apartment rentals are found in popular Wicker Park and Lincoln Park.

Useful Websites

Choose Chicago (www.choosechicago.com) Official tourist information site.

CTA (www.transitchicago.com) Bus and train maps, schedules and fares.

Chicago Reader (www.chicagoreader.com) Covers music, arts, restaurants and politics from an alternative perspective.

Road Trip Near Chicago: 3

Destination coverage: p77

St Louis Downtown skyline at twilight

ST LOUIS

Slide into St Louis and revel in the unique vibe of the largest city in the Great Plains. Beer, bowling and baseball are some of the top attractions, but history and culture are also a vital part of the fabric. Plus this old city by the river is a sensational place for food and nightlife.

Getting Around

If you're going out for a drink, Metro (www.metrostlouis.org) runs local buses and the MetroLink light-rail system (which connects the airport, the Loop, Central West End, the Gateway Transportation Center/Union Station and Downtown). Buses 30 and 40 serve Soulard from Downtown.

Where to Eat

St Louis boasts the region's most diverse selection of food, from the Irish pubs of Soulard to the Asian restaurants along South Grand. Don't leave town without sampling the city's unique approach to Italian American cuisine in The Hill.

Where to Stay

Most midrange and upscale chains have a hotel near the Gateway Arch in Downtown. Indie cheapies are thin on the ground in interesting areas, but you'll find some near the airport and you can ride the MetroLink light rail into the city.

Nightlife

Laclede's Landing, Soulard and the Loop are loaded with pubs and bars, many with live music. The Grove, a strip of Manchester Ave between Kingshighway Blvd and S Vandeventer Ave, is the hub of St Louis' LGBTIQ+ community.

Useful Websites

Explore St Louis. (www.explorestlouis.com) Excellent resource with local branches.

Missouri Division of Tourism (www.visitmo.com)

Sauce (www.saucemagazine.com) Website and magazine with great food and entertainment reviews.

Road Trip Through St Louis: 1

Destination coverage: p59

NEED TO KNOW

CELL PHONES

Foreign phones that operate on tri- or quad-band frequencies work in the USA. Otherwise, purchase cheap cell phones with a pay-as-you-go plan on arrival.

INTERNET ACCESS

Free wi-fi is found in hotels, cafes and some fast-food chains, but the smaller the town, the harder it is to find.

FUEL

Gas stations are everywhere, except in some remote desert and mountain areas.

RENTAL CARS

Avis (www.avis.com)

Enterprise (www.enterprise.com)

Hertz (www.hertz.com)

IMPORTANT NUMBERS

AAA (☎800-222-4357) Roadside assistance for auto-club members.

Emergency (☎911)

Directory Assistance (☎411)

Operator (☎0)

VISAS

See p121

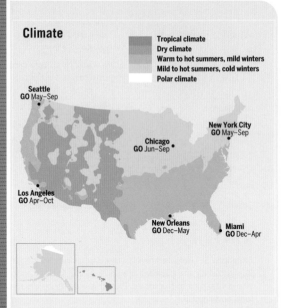

Climate

Tropical climate
Dry climate
Warm to hot summers, mild winters
Mild to hot summers, cold winters
Polar climate

Seattle
GO May–Sep

New York City
GO May–Sep

Chicago
GO Jun–Sep

Los Angeles
GO Apr–Oct

New Orleans
GO Dec–May

Miami
GO Dec–Apr

When to Go

High Season (Jun–Aug)

》 Warm days across the country, with generally high temperatures.

》 Busiest season, with big crowds and higher prices.

》 In ski-resort areas, January to March is high season.

Shoulder (Apr–May, Sep–Oct)

》 Milder temperatures, fewer crowds.

》 Spring flowers (April) and fiery autumn colors (October) in many parts of the country.

Low Season (Nov–Mar)

》 Wintery days, with snowfall in the north, and heavier rains in some regions.

》 Lowest prices for accommodations (aside from ski resorts and warmer getaway destinations).

Your Daily Budget

Budget: Less than $150

» Camping or hostel: $10–50; cheap motel room: $60–100

» Roadside diner or take-out meal: $6–15

Midrange: $150–250

» Midrange hotel room: $75–200

» Casual sit-down restaurant meal: $15–30

Top End: More than $250

» Resort hotel room: from $250

» Three-course meal in top restaurant: $60–100

Eating

Diners, drive-ins and cafes Cheap, simple and occasionally homemade food.

Seafood shacks Casual waterfront kitchens for fresh catch.

Brewpubs and gastropubs Regional craft beers and wines, 'pub grub' from hearty to high-end cuisine.

Vegetarians and other diets Food restrictions and allergies can often be catered for, especially in cities.

Price indicators refer to a main course; tax and tip usually are not included.

$ less than $15

$$ $15–$25

$$$ more than $25

Sleeping

Camping Ranging from amenity-rich RV parks to primitive wilderness sites.

Motels Everywhere along highways, around cities and in heavily touristed spots.

Hotels and hostels Common in metro areas and tourist hot spots.

B&Bs Smaller, often historical and romantic, but pricey.

Price indicators refer to a double room in high season, excluding taxes.

$ less than $150

$$ $150–$250

$$$ more than $250

Arriving in the USA

Major US airports offer free inter-terminal transportation and car-rental shuttles.

JFK International Airport (New York) From JFK take the AirTrain to Jamaica Station and then LIRR to Penn Station ($15 to $19; 45 minutes). A taxi to Manhattan costs around $60, plus toll and tip (45 to 90 minutes).

Los Angeles International Airport LAX Flyaway Bus to Union Station costs $9.75 (35 to 55 minutes). To Downtown a door-to-door Prime Time shuttle costs around $36 (35 to 75 minutes), a taxi around $60 (25 to 50 minutes).

Miami International Airport SuperShuttle to South Beach for $22 (50 to 90 minutes); taxi to South Beach for $35 (40 minutes); or take the Miami Beach Airport Express (bus 150) for $2.25, which makes stops from 41st to Miami Beach's southern tip.

Money

ATMs are widely available. Credit cards are accepted at most hotels, restaurants and shops, and usually are required for making reservations.

Tipping

Tipping is expected, not optional: 15% to 20% at restaurants and bars, 10% to 15% for taxi drivers, and $2 per bag for porters.

Useful Websites

Lonely Planet (www.lonelyplanet.com/usa) Destination information, hotel reviews and more.

Eater (www.eater.com) Foodie insight into two dozen US cities.

Roadside America (www.roadsideamerica.com) For all things weird and wacky.

Opening Hours

Opening hours may be shorter in winter (November to March).

Banks 8:30am–4:30pm Monday to Thursday, to 5:30pm Friday, some 9am–noon Saturday

Businesses and government offices 9am to 5pm Monday–Friday

Restaurants 7am–10:30am, 11:30am–2:30pm and 5pm–9pm, some later Friday and Saturday

Shops 9am–6pm Monday to Saturday, noon–5pm Sunday (malls later)

For more, see USA Driving guide (p109)

Road Trips

1 **Black Hills Loop** 2–3 Days
Icons, beauty and fun combine for the perfect driving loop. (p17)

2 **The Might Mo** 7 Days
America's longest river first lured Lewis and Clark, now it's your turn. (p27)

3 **Michigan's Gold Coast** 4 Days
A spin along Lake Michigan's shore features beaches, wineries and island-hopping. (p37)

4 **Highway 61** 2–3 Days
The Minnesota byway hugs Lake Superior's rugged edge, passing waterfalls and moose. (p47)

Mt Rushmore (p20)
CHRIS HIGGINS PHOTOGRAPHY/SHUTTERSTOCK ©

Black Hills Loop

1

Shaggy bison lumber across the plains. Giant monuments praise great men. Windswept prairies unfurl below towering mountains. This Black Hills tour embraces the region's heritage in all its messy glory.

TRIP HIGHLIGHTS

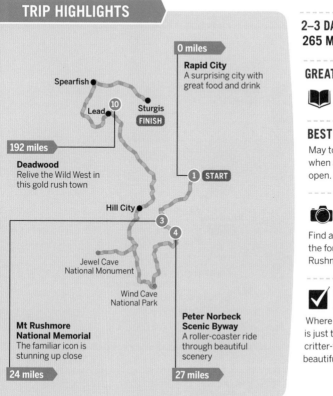

0 miles

Rapid City
A surprising city with great food and drink

Spearfish

10

Lead **Sturgis**
FINISH

192 miles

Deadwood
Relive the Wild West in this gold rush town

Hill City

1 **START**

3

4

Jewel Cave National Monument

Wind Cave National Park

Mt Rushmore National Memorial
The familiar icon is stunning up close

24 miles

Peter Norbeck Scenic Byway
A roller-coaster ride through beautiful scenery

27 miles

2–3 DAYS
265 MILES / 426KM

GREAT FOR...

BEST TIME TO GO
May to September, when all sights are open.

ESSENTIAL PHOTO
Find a new angle on the four mugs at Mt Rushmore.

✓ BEST FOR OUTDOORS
Where buffalo roam is just the start of critter-filled days amid beautiful scenery.

Crazy Horse Memorial (p24) Native American cultural performance

17

1 Black Hills Loop

In the early 1800s, 60 million buffalo roamed the plains. Rampant overhunting decimated their ranks and by 1889 fewer than 1000 remained. Today, their numbers have climbed to 500,000; several Black Hills parks manage healthy herds. On this tour you'll see the iconic buffalo and other legendary sights, including the Badlands, Mt Rushmore, the Crazy Horse Memorial, sprawling parks and the town made famous for having no law: Deadwood.

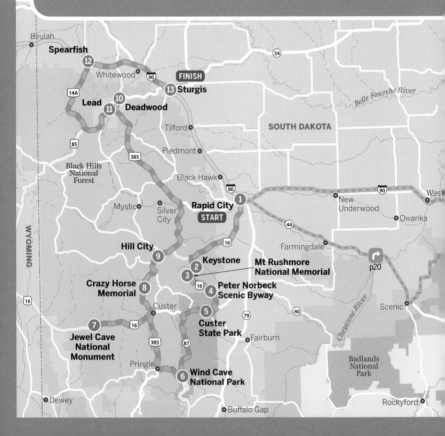

❶ Rapid City

A worthy capital to the region, 'Rapid' has an intriguing, lively and walkable downtown. Well-preserved brick buildings, filled with quality shops and places to dine, make it a good urban base and hub for your looping tour. Get a walking-tour brochure of Rapid's historic buildings and public art from the visitor center. Check out the watery fun on **Main St Square**.

Cheyenne River

Wall

280 miles to
2

(14) Cottonwood

(90)

Buffalo Gap
National
Grassland

dlands
tional
Park

(240)

Cedar
Pass

(44) White River

(44)

Pine Ridge Indian
Reservation

While strolling, don't miss the **Statues of Presidents** (www.presidentsrc.com; 631 Main St; ⊙ info center noon-9pm Mon-Sat May-Sep, shorter hours other times) on downtown street corners. From a shifty-eyed Nixon in repose to a triumphant Harry Truman, lifelike statues dot corners throughout the center. Collect all 44.

Learn about how dramatic natural underground events over the eons have produced some spectacular rocks. See these plus dinosaur bones and some stellar fossils at the **Museum of Geology** (☏605-394-2467; http://museum.sdsmt.edu; 501 E St Joseph St, O'Harra Bldg; ⊙9am-6pm Mon-Sat Jun-Aug, 8:30am-4pm Mon-Sat Sep-May), located at the South Dakota School of Mines & Technology.

The Drive ⟫ Choose from the commercial charms on Hwys 16 and 16A on the 21-mile drive to Keystone.

❷ Keystone

One indisputable fact about the Black Hills?

It will always, always, always take longer than you think to reach a key attraction. Trust us. Slow-moving Winnebagos, serpentine byways and kitschy roadside distractions will deaden your pace. And the distractions start early on Hwy 16 where family-friendly and delightfully hokey tourist attractions vie for dollars on the way to Mt Rushmore, including the animal-happy **Bear Country USA** (☏605-343-2290; www.bearcountryusa.com; 13820 US 16; adult/child $18/12; ⊙8am-6pm May-Aug, reduced hours Sep-Nov; 👪) and **Reptile Gardens** (☏800-335-0275; www.reptilegardens.com; 8955 Hwy 16; adult/child $18/12; ⊙8am-5pm Jun-Aug, 9am-4pm Sep, Oct & Mar-May; 👪).

Kitsch reigns supreme in Keystone, a gaudy town bursting with rah-rah patriotism, Old West spirit and too many fudgeries. The fuss is directly attributable to its proximity to Mt Rushmore, 3 miles west.

The Drive ⟫ It's a mere 3-mile jaunt uphill to Mt Rushmore.

LINK YOUR TRIP

2 **The Mighty Mo**
Follow North America's longest river through magnificent wilderness and great cities.

Join the route in Pierre, SD, a 170-mile trip east of Rapid City via I-90 plus a scenic leg on US 14.

Keep yours eyes peeled for the first glimpse of a president.

- - - - - - - - - - - - - - - - -

TRIP HIGHLIGHT

③ Mt Rushmore National Memorial

Glimpses of Washington's nose from the roads leading to this hugely popular monument never cease to surprise and are but harbingers of the full impact of this mountainside sculpture once you're up close (and past the less impressive parking area and entrance walk). George Washington, Thomas Jefferson, Abraham Lincoln and Theodore Roosevelt each iconically stare into the distance in 60ft-tall granite glory.

It's hugely popular, but you can easily escape the crowds and fully appreciate **Mt Rushmore** (☎605-574-2523; www.nps.gov/moru; off Hwy 244; parking $10; ⏰5am-11pm Jun-Aug, to 9pm Sep, much shorter hours other times) while marveling at the artistry of sculptor Gutzon Borglum and the immense labor of the workers who created the memorial between 1927 and 1941.

The **Presidential Trail** loop passes right below the monument for some fine nostril views and gives you access to the worthwhile **Sculptor's Studio**. Start clockwise and you're right under Washington's nose in less than five minutes. The **nature trail** to the right as you face the entrance

---

↱ DETOUR:
BADLANDS NATIONAL PARK & MORE

Start: ① Rapid City

More than 600 buffalo, also known as North American bison, roam **Badlands National Park** (☎605-433-5361; www.nps.gov/badl; Hwy 240; 7-day park pass bicycle/car $15/30). The name originated with French trappers and the Lakota Sioux, who described the park's jagged spires and crumbling buttes as 'bad lands.' Today, this crumbling former floodplain is visually compelling, its corrugated hillsides enlivened by an ever-changing palette of reds and pinks.

You can see the eroding rocks up close on the **Notch Trail**, a 1.5-mile (round-trip) leg stretcher that twists through a canyon, scampers up a wooden ladder then curves along a crumbly ridgeline to an expansive view of grasslands and more serrated walls. At the **Ben Reifel Visitor Center** (⏰7am-7pm Jun-Aug, 8am-5pm Apr, May, Sep & Oct, 8am-4pm Nov-Mar) just down the road, a visually stunning film captures the park's natural diversity with jaw-dropping close-ups of the plants and animals that thrive in the mixed-grass prairie.

From Rapid City, head about 50 miles east on I-90, where **Badlands Loop Rd** (Hwy 240) links with I-90 at exits 131 and 110. The loop stretches west from the visitor center into the park's north unit, curving along a narrow ridge of buttes known as the **Badlands Wall**. It can be driven in an hour, but stopping at the numerous overlooks can easily fill a morning. Exit 110 off I-90 also serves Wall, home to the eponymous **Wall Drug** (☎605-279-2175; www.walldrug.com; 510 Main St; ⏰8am-8pm; ♿), one of the world's great – and unmissable – tourist traps.

To avoid I-90 back to Rapid City, pick up Hwy 44, which can be accessed at several points from the Badlands. Jagged bluffs give way to rolling prairie on this made-for-convertibles byway that swings through the **Buffalo Gap National Grassland** on its way west.

connects the viewing and parking areas, passing through a pine forest and avoiding the crowds and commercialism.

The official National Park Service **information center** has an excellent bookstore with proceeds going to the park. Avoid the schlocky Xanterra gift shop and the disappointing Carvers Cafe, which looked much better in the scene where Cary Grant gets plugged in *North by Northwest*. The main **museum** is far from comprehensive but the fascinating Sculptor's Studio conveys the drama of how the monument came to be.

The Drive » Backtrack slightly from Mt Rushmore and head southwest for 16 miles of thrills on Iron Mountain Rd.

TRIP HIGHLIGHT

4 Peter Norbeck Scenic Byway

Driving the 66-mile Peter Norbeck Scenic Byway is like flirting with a brand-new crush: always exhilarating, occasionally challenging and sometimes you get a few butterflies. Named for the South Dakota senator who pushed for its creation in 1919, the oval-shaped byway is broken into four roads linking the most memorable destinations in the Black Hills (drivers of large RVs should call Custer State Park for tunnel measurements).

Iron Mountain Rd (Hwy 16A) is the real star, beloved for its pigtailing loops, Mt Rushmore–framing tunnels and one gorgeous glide through sun-dappled pines. It's a 16-mile roller coaster of wooden bridges, virtual loop-the-loops, narrow tunnels and stunning vistas. Expect lots of drivers going even slower than you are.

The 14-mile **Needles Hwy** (Hwy 87) swoops below granite spires, careens past rocky overlooks and slings though a supernarrow tunnel.

The Drive » Once past the Iron Mountain Rd, other Peter Norbeck Scenic Byway options aside, it is only 3 miles along Hwy 16 west to the Custer State Park visitor center.

-----

5 Custer State Park

The only reason 111-sq-mile **Custer State Park** (☏605-255-4515; https://gfp.sd.gov/parks/detail/custer-state-park; 7-day pass per car $20; ⊙24hr) isn't a national park is that the state grabbed it first. It boasts one of the largest free-roaming bison herds in the world (about 1500), the famous 'begging burros' (donkeys seeking handouts) and more than 200 bird species. Other wildlife include elk, pronghorns, mountain goats, bighorn sheep, coyotes, prairie dogs, mountain lions and bobcats. Meandering over

awesome stone bridges and across sublime alpine meadows, the 18-mile **Wildlife Loop Road** allows plenty of spotting.

The **Custer State Park Visitor Center** (https://gfp.sd.gov/csp-visitor-center; junction US 16A & Wildlife Loop Rd; ⊙9am-6pm Jun-Sep, to 4pm Oct-May), situated on the eastern side of the park, contains good exhibits and offers guided nature walks. The nearby **Black Hills Playhouse** (☏605-255-4141; www.blackhillsplayhouse.com; 24834 S Playhouse Rd, off Hwy 87; tickets adult/child $35/16; ⊙schedule varies Jun–mid-Aug) hosts summer theater.

Hiking through the pine-covered hills and prairie grassland is a great way to see wildlife and rock formations. Trails through **Sylvan Lake Shore**, **Sunday Gulch**, **Cathedral Spires** and **French Creek Natural Area** are all highly recommended.

The park is named for the notorious George A Custer, who led a scientific expedition into the Black Hills in 1874. The expedition's discovery of gold drew so many new settlers that an 1868 treaty granting the Sioux a 60-million-acre reservation in the area was eventually broken. Crazy Horse and the Lakotas retaliated, killing Custer and 265 of his men at Montana's Battle of the Little Big Horn in 1876.

WHY THIS IS A CLASSIC TRIP
MARK JOHANSON, WRITER

Ride the roller-coaster roads into the pine-covered Black Hills, and the golden plains of the American heartland seem a world away. Iconic Mt Rushmore lures most visitors to this remote region, but it's the prismatic caves, herds of bison and Wild West tales of Deadwood's larger-than-life characters that leave lasting memories. Hike or bike near attractive resort towns, then laze away an afternoon in a bubbling thermal spring.

Above: Bison herd, Custer State Park (p21)
Left: Deadwood (p24)
Right: Mt Rushmore National Memorial (p20)

PAUL R. JONES/SHUTTERSTOCK ©

The Drive » Near the western edge of Custer State Park, head due south on Hwy 87 for 19 miles from US 16. It's a beautiful ride through a long swath of wilderness and park.

---

6 Wind Cave National Park

This **park** (📞605-745-4600; www.nps.gov/wica; off US 385; admission free; 🕐 visitor center 8am-7pm Jun–mid-Aug, reduced hours mid-Aug–May), protecting 44 sq miles of grassland and forest, sits just south of Custer State Park. The central feature is, of course, the cave, which contains 147 miles of mapped passages. The cave's foremost feature is its 'boxwork' calcite formations (95% of all that are known exist here), which look like honeycomb and date back 60 to 100 million years. The strong gusts of wind that are felt at the entrance, but not inside, give the cave its name. The Covid-19 pandemic put a damper on tours, but luckily, not all of the park's treasures are underground. Wind Cave's above-ground acres abound with bison and prairie dogs.

The Drive » Scenic drives continue as you go from one big hole in the ground to another. Jewel Cave is 38 miles northwest on US 385 and US 16.

7 Jewel Cave National Monument

Another of the Black Hills' many fascinating caves is **Jewel Cave** ([☎]605-673-8300; www.nps.gov/jeca; off US 16; [☺]visitor center 8am-5:30pm Jun-Sep, 8:30am-4:30pm Oct-May), 13 miles west of Custer on US 16, so named because calcite crystals line many of its walls. Currently 187 miles have been surveyed (3% of the estimated total), making it the third-longest known cave in the world. You can check at the visitor center if tours (fees apply) are happening (they were paused due to the Covid-19 pandemic). If not, try one of the trails that depart right outside of the center.

The Drive » Retrace your route for 13 miles until US 385 joins US 16 and then go north for 5 miles.

8 Crazy Horse Memorial

The world's largest monument, the **Crazy Horse Memorial** ([☎]605-673-4681; www.crazyhorsememorial.org; 12151 Ave of the Chiefs, off US 385; per person/car $12/30; [☺]8am-9pm Jun-Sep, reduced hours Oct-May) is a 563ft-tall work-in-progress. When finished it will depict the Sioux leader astride his horse, pointing to

the horizon saying, 'My lands are where my dead lie buried.'

Never photographed or persuaded to sign a meaningless treaty, Crazy Horse was chosen for a monument that Lakota Sioux elders hoped would balance the presidential focus of Mt Rushmore. In 1948 a Boston-born sculptor, the indefatigable Korczak Ziolkowski, started blasting granite. His family have continued the work since his death in 1982. (It should be noted that many Native Americans oppose the monument as desecration of sacred land.)

No one is predicting when the sculpture will be complete (the face was dedicated in 1998). A rather thrilling laser-light show tells the tales of the monument on summer evenings.

The visitor center complex includes a Native American museum, a cultural center, cafes and Ziolkowski's studio.

The Drive » It's a short 10-mile drive north on US 16/385 to the refreshments of Hill City.

9 Hill City

One of the most appealing towns up in the hills, Hill City (www.hillcitysd.com) is less frenzied than places such as Keystone. Its main drag has cafes and galleries.

1880 Train ([☎]605-574-2222; www.1880train.com; 222 Railroad Ave, Hill City; adult/child round-trip $32/16; [☺]mid-May–Dec) is a classic steam train running through rugged country to and from Keystone. An interesting train **museum** is next door.

The Drive » Lakes, rivers, meadows and a few low-key tourist traps enliven the 42 miles on US 385 to Deadwood through the heart of the Black Hills.

TRIP HIGHLIGHT

10 Deadwood

Fans of the iconic HBO TV series may recall that Deadwood was the epitome of lawlessness in the 1870s. Today things have changed, although the 80 gambling halls, big and small, would no doubt put a sly grin on the faces of the hard characters who founded the town.

Deadwood's atmospheric streets are lined with gold-rush-era buildings lavishly restored with gambling dollars. Its storied past is easy to find at its museums and cemeteries. There's eternal devotion to Wild Bill Hickok, who was shot in the back of the head here in 1876 while gambling.

Actors reenact famous **shootouts** (Main St; [☺]2pm, 4pm & 6pm Mon-Sat Jun–mid-Sep) on Main St during summer, including the

1877 saloon fight between Tom Smith and David Lunt (who lived for 67 days relatively unbothered by the bullet in his head before finally dropping dead).

The Drive » Lead is just 4 miles uphill from Deadwood, through land scarred by generations hunting for gold.

⑪ Lead

Lead (pronounced 'leed') has slowly gentrifying charm but still bears plenty of scars from the mining era. Gape at the 1250ft-deep open-pit mine from the **Sanford Lab Homestake Visitor Center** (☏605-584-3110; www.sanfordlabhomestake. com; 160 W Main St; viewing area free, tours adult/child $10/8; ⊙9am-5pm) to see what open-pit mining can do to a mountain.

Nearby are the same mine's shafts, which plunge more than 1.5 miles below the surface and are now being used for physics research.

The Drive » Climb out of steep canyons for 11 miles on US 14A until you plunge back down into Spearfish Canyon.

⑫ Spearfish

Spearfish Canyon Scenic Byway (www.spearfish canyon.com/scenicby way) is a waterfall-lined, curvaceous 20-mile road that cleaves from the heart of the hills into Spearfish. There's a sight worth stopping for around every bend; pause for longer than a minute and you'll hear beavers hard at work.

The Drive » It's a quick 22 miles east on I-90 to Sturgis. That solitary headlight in the

rearview mirror is a hog hoping to blow past. From Sturgis back to Rapid City is only 36 miles.

⑬ Sturgis

Neon-lit tattoo parlors, Christian iconography and billboards for ribald biker bars featuring dolled-up models are just some of the cacophony of images of this loud and proud biker town. Shop for leather on Main St, don your American flag bandana and sidle up to the saloon bar to give a toast to the stars and stripes.

Things get even louder for the annual **Sturgis Motorcycle Rally** (☏605-720-0800; www.sturgismotor cyclerally.com; ⊙early Aug), when around 700,000 riders, fans and curious onlookers take over the town.

The Mighty Mo

Follow the course of North America's longest river as it runs past great cities, evocative wilderness and sites embedded in US history.

TRIP HIGHLIGHTS

**7 DAYS
1388 MILES /
2234KM**

GREAT FOR...

BEST TIME TO GO

May to September, when all the sights are open.

ESSENTIAL PHOTO

Any shot that shows the Missouri River's impressive girth.

BEST FOR HISTORY

Much of the USA's 19th-century sense of self was formed by events along the river.

13 FINISH

12 Bismarck

1388 miles
Williston
The Missouri meets the Yellowstone in a mighty river confluence

1219 miles
Stanton
Visit the village site where Lewis and Clark met Sacagawea

Pierre

Sioux City

Omaha

309 miles
Kansas City
Jazz, barbecue and great neighborhoods make KC hard to leave

4

START 1

0 miles
St Louis
The landmark arch recalls Lewis and Clark and their adventure west

2 The Mighty Mo

In 1804–05, Lewis and Clark followed the Missouri River during the first stages of their legendary journey west. With their Corps of Discovery, they canoed up the river, meeting Native Americans – some friendly, others hostile – and discovering vast expanses of land, untouched for eons and teeming with wildlife. Exploring the river today, you can make your very own discoveries.

TRIP HIGHLIGHT

1 St Louis

Fur-trapper Pierre Laclede knew prime real estate when he saw it, putting down stakes at the junction of the Mississippi and Missouri Rivers in 1764. The hustle picked up considerably when prospectors discovered gold in California in 1848 and St Louis (p59) became the jumping-off point first for get-rich-quick dreamers and later for waves of settlers. Its unique position made it the 'Gateway to the West.'

As a symbol for the city, the **Gateway Arch** (☎877-982-1410; www.gatewayarch.com; 11 N 4th St; tram ride adult/child from $12/8; ⊘ grounds 5am-11pm, Arch by reservation 8am-10pm Jun-Aug, 9am-6pm Sep-May, last tram 1hr before closing; 🚻) has soared above any expectations its backers could have had in 1965 when it opened. The centerpiece of this National Park Service complex, the silvery, shimmering 630ft-high arch is the Great Plains' own Eiffel Tower. A tram ride takes you to the tight confines at the top.

The arch sits atop a revitalized **museum** (www.nps.gov/jeff; Gateway Arch; adult/child $3/free; ⊘8am-10pm Jun-Aug, 9am-6pm Sep-May; 🚻) that explains the vision of Thomas Jefferson, who sponsored the Lewis and Clark expedition. It began here on May 14, 1804, and followed the Missouri River, much as you'll do on this tour. It offers a balanced view of what western expansion meant for the Native Americans living on the lands and the newly arrived pioneers.

The Drive » To use a cliché, from the arch, go west (about 24 miles on busy I-70).

---

2 St Charles

This Missouri River town, founded in 1769, has a cobblestoned Main St. Within the well-preserved downtown you can visit the **First State**

LINK YOUR TRIP

1 Black Hills Loop
Great sights, including Mt Rushmore, await in South Dakota's beautiful Black Hills. Start in Rapid City, SD, a 170-mile trip west of Pierre.

Capitol (☎636-940-3322; https://mostateparks.com/park/first-missouri-state-capitol-state-historic-site; 200 S Main St; tours adult/child $4.50/3; ☺10am-4pm Tue-Sat year-round, 10am-4pm Mon Apr-Oct, noon-4pm Sun Mar-Dec). Ask at the **visitor center** (☎800-366-2427; www.discoverstcharles.com; 230 S Main St; ☺8am-5pm Mon-Fri, from 10am Sat, from noon Sun) about tours, which pass some rare French colonial architecture in the **Frenchtown neighborhood** just north.

Clark joined Lewis here and they began their epic journey on May 21, 1804. Their encampment is reenacted annually on that date. The **Lewis & Clark Boathouse & Nature Center** (☎636-947-3199; www.lewisandclark center.org; 1050 S Riverside Dr; adult/child $5/2; ☺10am-5pm Mon-Sat, from noon Sun) has displays about the duo and replicas of their boats.

The Drive ≫ Skip the elusive charms of I-70 and instead stay close to the river, taking first Hwy 94 and then cutting north via Columbia (which has good cafes downtown) on US 63. From here take Hwy 740, Hwy 240, US 40 and Hwy 41 in that order for a total journey of 190 miles.

---

❸ Arrow Rock

Perched just above and west of the Missouri River, **Arrow Rock State Historic Site** (☎660-837-3330; www.mostateparks.com/park/arrow-rock-state-historic-site; off Hwy 41; campsites from $13; ☺park 7am-10pm, visitor center 10am-4pm daily Mar-Nov, Fri-Sun Dec-Feb)

↪ DETOUR: HANNIBAL

Start: ❷ St Charles

Hannibal is on that *other* river, the Mississippi. When the air is sultry in this old river town, you almost expect to hear the whistle of a paddle steamer. Mark Twain's boyhood home, 100 miles northwest of St Louis, has some authentically vintage areas and plenty of sites where you can get a sense of the muse and his creations, Tom Sawyer and Huck Finn.

The **Mark Twain Boyhood Home & Museum** (☎573-221-9010; www.marktwainmuseum.org; 120 N Main St; adult/child $12/6; ☺10am-5pm mid-Mar–Dec, to 4pm Jan–mid-Mar; ♿) presents eight buildings, including two homes Twain lived in and that of Laura Hawkins, the real-life inspiration for Becky Thatcher. Afterward, float down the Mississippi on the **Mark Twain Riverboat** (☎573-221-3222; www.marktwainriverboat.com; Center St Landing; 1hr sightseeing cruise adult/child $21/12; ☺Apr-Nov, schedule varies). **National Tom Sawyer Days** (www.hannibaljaycees.org; ☺weekend near Jul 4) feature frog-jumping and fence-painting contests and much more.

From St Charles, Hannibal is 95 miles northwest through low, rolling hills via US 61.

Kansas City The Missouri and Kansas Rivers meet in the city

is a small preserved town that feels little changed since the 1830s when it was on the main stagecoach route west.

The Drive » Hwy 41 followed by US 65 and US 24 take you through rolling Missouri countryside and after 95 miles right into the heart of Kansas City.

TRIP HIGHLIGHT

④ Kansas City

Kansas City (KC; p65) began life in 1821 as a trading post but really came into its own once westward expansion began. The Oregon, California and Santa Fe Trails all met steamboats loaded with pioneers here.

KC is famed for its barbecues (100-plus joints smoke it up), fountains (more than 200; on par with Rome) and jazz.

Neighborhoods not to miss include: **River Market**, home to hipster spots, immediately north of downtown; and **Westport**, located on Westport Rd, just west of Main St, filled with alluring locally owned restaurants and bars. Hit the **Kaw Point Park** (☎913-677-2088; www. lewisandclarkwyco.org; 1403 Fairfax Trafficway; ☺dawn-dusk) at the confluence of the Missouri and Kansas Rivers where Lewis and Clark passed in 1804.

The unpredictable Missouri River claimed hundreds of riverboats. At the **Arabia Steamboat Museum** (☎816-471-1856; www.1856.com; 400 Grand Blvd; adult/child $14.50/5.50; ☺10am-5pm Mon-Sat, from noon Sun, last tour 3:30pm) you can see 200 tons of salvaged 'treasure' from an 1856 victim. In nearby Independence, don't miss the National Frontier Trails Museum, which details the hardships on a wagon train.

31

The Drive » Quickly escape KC's endless suburbs by darting north 55 miles on I-29.

---

⑤ St Joseph

The first Pony Express set out in 1860, carrying mail from 'St Jo' 2000 miles west to California, taking just eight days. The service lasted 18 months before telegraph lines made it redundant. The **Pony Express National Museum** (☎816-279-5059; www.ponyexpress.org; 914 Penn St; adult/child $7/3; ⏱9am-5pm Mon-Sat, 11am-4pm Sun) tells the story of the dangerous Express and its riders.

St Jo, just east of the Missouri River, was home to outlaw Jesse James. He was killed at what is now the **Patee House Museum** (☎816-232-8206; www.ponyexpressjessejames.com; 1202 Penn St; adult/child $7/5; ⏱9am-4pm Mon-Sat, from noon Sun; ♿). The fateful bullet hole is still in the wall.

Housed in the former 'State Lunatic Asylum No 2,' the **Glore Psychiatric Museum** (☎816-232-8471; www.stjosephmuseum.org; 3406 Frederick Ave; adult/child $7/5; ⏱10am-5pm Mon-Sat, from 1pm Sun) gives a frightening and fascinating look at lobotomies, the 'bath of surprise' and other discredited treatments.

The Drive » Cross west to Nebraska on US 36 and then head north on US 75. While on this 157-mile-long leg, look for views of the Missouri from old river towns like Nebraska City.

---

⑥ Omaha

Home to the brick-and-cobblestoned **Old Market** neighborhood downtown, a lively music scene and several quality museums, Omaha can turn a few hours into a few days.

Omaha's location on the Missouri River and proximity to the Platte made it an important stop on the Oregon, California and Mormon Trails. Later, the first transcontinental railroad to California stretched west from here. Its history is recounted at the **Union Pacific Railroad Museum** (☎712-329-8307; www.uprrmuseum.org; 200 Pearl St, Council Bluffs; ⏱by reservation 10am-4pm Thu-Sat; ♿) in nearby Council Bluffs.

The downtown **riverfront** (8th St & Riverfront Dr) offers many walking routes and sights. Among the highlights: the architecturally stunning **Bob Kerrey Pedestrian Bridge** (705 Riverfront Dr), which soars over to Iowa; the **Heartland of America Park** (800 Douglas St), with fountains and lush gardens; and **Lewis & Clark Landing** (345 Riverfront Dr), where the explorers did just that in 1804. It's home to the **Lewis & Clark National Historical Trail Visitor Center** (☎402-661-1804; www.nps.gov/lecl; 601 Riverfront Dr; ⏱8am-5pm Mon-Fri, from 9:30am Sat & Sun May-Oct, 8am-4:30pm Mon-Fri Nov-Apr), where you can get information and advice for following in their footsteps.

The Drive » Just beyond the outer reaches of ever-growing Omaha, Fort Calhoun is 16 miles north on US 75.

---

⑦ Fort Calhoun

The small town of Fort Calhoun has a sight that takes you back to days long gone on the Missouri. **Fort Atkinson State Historical Park** (☎402-468-5611; www.fortatkinsononline.org; 201 S 7th St, Fort Calhoun; park per vehicle $8, visitor center adult/child $2/1; ⏱park 8am-5pm, visitor center 10am-5pm Jun-Aug, Sat & Sun May & Sep) preserves the first US military fort built west of the Missouri River. It was built in 1820 on a recommendation of Lewis and Clark, who, besides being explorers, were keen military officers.

The Drive » Farm towns hoping to be remembered by time dot the 84 miles of US 75 north from Fort Calhoun. The road's general route gently bends with the overall course of the Missouri River to the east.

---

⑧ Sioux City

On a high bluff, the modest city of Sioux City, IA, has grand views looking west over the Missouri

River. There's a good **overlook** at the corner of W Fourth and Burton Sts.

On August 20, 1804, Sergeant Charles Floyd became the only person to die on the Lewis and Clark expedition team, probably from appendicitis. You can learn much more about this and other aspects of the journey at the beautiful **Lewis & Clark Interpretive Center** (☏712-224-5242; www.siouxcitylcic.com; 900 Larsen Park Rd, near I-29 exit 149; ⊙9am-5pm Tue-Fri, from noon Sat & Sun; ♿), which is right on the river.

The Drive ›› Enjoy the smallest of rural two-laners to reach the first capitol of the Dakota states. Angle out of Sioux City on Hwy 12, then cross over to South Dakota at Westfield and pick up the alternately sinuous and angular Hwy 50, which closely follows the river. The final 64 miles of this 306-mile-long leg are on Hwy 34.

- - - - - - - - - - - - - - - - -

❾ Pierre

Pierre (pronounced 'peer'), SD, is just too small (population 14,100) and ordinary to feel like a seat of power. Small-town Victorian homes overlook the imposing 1910 **State Capitol** (☏605-773-3688; www.boa.sd.gov/capitol; 500 E Capitol Ave; ⊙8am-6pm Mon-Fri, to 5pm Sat & Sun) with its black copper dome.

Hard by the Missouri River, it lies along the

DETOUR: MITCHELL

Start: ❽ **Sioux City**

Why not honor the starch you'll see growing in profusion in vibrant green fields all along the Missouri? Every year, half a million people pull off I-90 (exit 332) to see the Taj Mahal of agriculture, the all-time-ultimate roadside attraction, the **Corn Palace** (☏605-995-8430; www.cornpalace.com; 604 N Main St; ⊙8am-9pm Jun-Aug, reduced hours Sep-May). Close to 300,000 ears of corn are used each year to create a tableaux of murals on the outside of the building. Ponder the scenes and you may find a kernel of truth or just say 'aw shucks.' Head inside to see photos of how the facade has evolved over the years.

Mitchell is 150 miles northwest of Sioux City via I-29 and I-90. Rejoin the drive at Pierre, 150 miles northwest via I-90 and US 83.

Native American Scenic Byway and lonely, stark **US 14**. Imagine this area when it was rich with bison, beavers, elk and much more.

Exhibits at the **South Dakota Cultural Heritage Center** (☏605-773-3458; www.history.sd.gov; 900 Governors Dr; adult/child $4/free; ⊙9am-6:30pm Mon-Sat, 1-4:30pm Sun Jun-Aug, to 4:30pm Sep-May) include a bloody Ghost Dance shirt from the Battle of Wounded Knee.

At a bend on the river, **Framboise Island** has several hiking trails and plentiful wildlife. It's across from where the Lewis and Clark expedition spent four days in late September, 1804. The expedition was nearly derailed when they

inadvertently offended members of the local Brule tribe.

The Drive ›› Dams cause the Missouri to look like a lake for much of the 208 miles you'll drive north along US 83 to the other Dakota capitol.

- - - - - - - - - - - - - - - - -

❿ Bismarck

Compared with the sylvan charms of Pierre, the stark 1930s **State Capitol** (☏701-328-2480; 600 E Boulevard Ave, Capitol Hill; ⊙8am-4pm Mon-Fri, from 9am Sat, from 1pm Sun Jun-Aug, 9am-4pm Mon-Fri Sep-May, tours hourly except noon) in Bismarck, ND, is often referred to as the 'skyscraper of the prairie' and looks like a Stalinist school of dentistry.

Behind the statue of Sacagawea (a Native

American woman whose friendship proved invaluable to Lewis and Clark), the huge **North Dakota Heritage Center** (📞701-328-2666; https://state museum.nd.gov; 612 East Boulevard Ave, Capitol Hill; ⏱9am-4pm Mon-Fri, from 11am Sat & Sun) has details on everything from Norwegian bachelor farmers to the scores of nuclear bombs perched on missiles in silos across the state.

Fort Abraham Lincoln State Park (📞701-667-6340; www.parkrec.nd.gov/fort-abraham-lincoln-state-park; off Hwy 1806; per vehicle $7, tours adult/child $8/5; ⏱park 9am-5pm), 7 miles south of nearby Mandan on SR 1806, is well worth the detour. Its **On-a-Slant Indian Village** has five recreated Mandan earth lodges, while the fort, with several replica buildings, was Custer's last stop before the Battle of Little Bighorn.

The Drive 》 Maybe pancakes are popular in North Dakota because that's how flat much of the land is. See for yourself on this 40-mile drive north on US 83.

----

⑪ Washburn

There are several worthwhile attractions near the spot where Lewis and Clark wintered with the Mandan in 1804–05. Learn about the duo's expedition and the Native Americans who helped them at the **Lewis &**

Clark Interpretive Center (📞701-462-8535; www.parkrec.nd.gov/lewis-clark-interpretive-center; junction US 83 & ND Hwy 200A, Washburn; adult/child $8/5; ⏱interpretive center 10am-5pm Apr-Sep, 10am-5pm Mon-Sat Oct-Mar, fort 10am-5pm Tue-Sun Apr-Sep).

Fort Mandan, a replica of the fort built by Lewis and Clark, is 2.5 miles west (10 miles downstream from the flooded original site). It sits on a lonely stretch of the Missouri River marked by a monument to Seaman, the expedition's dog.

The Drive 》 Head 22 miles west of Washburn through verdant rolling prairie on Hwy 200 to just north of the small town of Stanton, ND.

TRIP HIGHLIGHT

⑫ Stanton

At **Knife River Indian Villages National Historical Site** (📞701-745-3300; www.nps.gov/knri; off Hwy 200; ⏱buildings 9am-5pm Jun-Aug, 8am-4:30pm Sep-May, trails dawn-dusk) you can still see the mounds left by three earthen villages of the Hidastas, who lived on the Knife River, a narrow tributary of the Missouri, for more than 900 years. The National Park Service has recreated one of the earthen lodges. A stroll through the mostly wide-open and wild site leads to the village where Lewis and Clark met Sacagawea.

The Drive 》 More dams cause the Missouri to balloon out into a tangle of waters that look like a couple of lizards doing a mating dance. Hwy 200 takes you for most of the 169 miles of your final leg.

TRIP HIGHLIGHT

⑬ Williston

Twenty-two miles southwest of Williston along SR 1804, **Fort Buford State Historic Site** (📞701-572-9034; www.history.nd.gov/historicsites/buford; Hwy 1804; adult/child $5/2.50; ⏱visitor center 9am-6pm Central Time, fort 10am-6pm Jun-Aug) preserves the bleak army outpost where Sitting Bull surrendered. The adjacent **Missouri-Yellowstone Confluence Interpretive Center** includes the fort's visitor center and has good views of where the Yellowstone River joins the Missouri.

About 2 miles west, on the Montana–North Dakota border, the moody and evocative **Fort Union Trading Post** (📞701-572-9083; www.nps.gov/fous; Hwy 1804; ⏱8am-6:30pm Central Time Jun-Aug, 9am-5pm Sep-May) is a reconstruction of the American Fur Company post built in 1828.

Over the border in Montana, the Missouri frays out into myriad tributaries. Lewis and Clark had numerous portages as they continued their epic journey west.

Right Fort Mandan

Michigan's Gold Coast

3

They don't call it the Gold Coast for nothing. Michigan's western shoreline features endless stretches of beaches, dunes, wineries, orchards and inn-filled towns that boom in summer.

TRIP HIGHLIGHTS

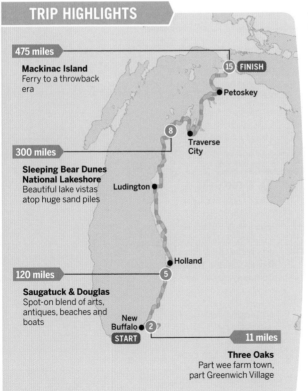

475 miles

Mackinac Island
Ferry to a throwback era

15 FINISH

● Petoskey

8

● Traverse City

300 miles

Sleeping Bear Dunes National Lakeshore
Beautiful lake vistas atop huge sand piles

Ludington ●

● Holland

120 miles

5

Saugatuck & Douglas
Spot-on blend of arts, antiques, beaches and boats

New Buffalo ● **2**
START

11 miles

Three Oaks
Part wee farm town, part Greenwich Village

**4 DAYS
475 MILES / 765KM**

GREAT FOR...

BEST TIME TO GO

July through October for pleasant weather and orchard harvests.

ESSENTIAL PHOTO

Atop the Dune Climb at Sleeping Bear Dunes.

BEST FOR FOODIES

Traverse City has artisan food shops selling local wines, ciders and produce.

Ludington State Park Big Sable Point Lighthouse (p42)

3 Michigan's Gold Coast

While Michigan's shore has been a holiday hot spot for over a century, it still surprises: the Caribbean-blue water, the West Coast surfing vibe, the French-style cider house that pops up by the road. Ernest Hemingway used to spend summers in the northern reaches, and he never forgot it. Even after traveling the world, he once wrote that the best sky is in northern Michigan in the fall.

1 New Buffalo

Hit the waves first in New Buffalo, a busy little resort town that is home to the Midwest's first surf shop. Yes, you can surf Lake Michigan, and the folks at **Third Coast Surf Shop** (269-932-4575; www.thirdcoastsurfshop.com; 110 N Whittaker St; 10am-7pm Sun-Wed, to 8pm Thu-Sat Jun-Aug, reduced hours Apr-May & Sep-Dec, closed Jan-Mar) will show you how. It rents wetsuits and boards ($20 to $30 per half day). For novices, it offers 1½-hour private lessons ($75, including equipment) at the local beach.

Not a surfer? Not a problem. Lounge on the wide, sandy beach; watch boats glide in and out of the marina; and lick an ice-cream cone or three.

The Drive » Follow Hwy 12 as it curves inland for 6 miles to the wee town of Three Oaks.

TRIP HIGHLIGHT

2 Three Oaks

Three Oaks is where Green Acres meets Greenwich Village in a bohemian farm-and-arts blend. Rent bikes at **Dewey Cannon Trading Company** (269-756-3361; www.facebook.com/deweycannontradingcompany; 3 Dewey Cannon Ave; bikes per day $15-$25; 10am-5pm Wed-Sun May-Oct, reduced hours Nov-Apr) and cycle lightly used roads past orchards and vineyards.

In the evening, catch a provocative play or art-house flick at Three Oaks' theaters.

Or just swing by for an hour or two to putter around the antiques stores and concrete-lawn-ornament shops. Be sure to stop in at **Journeyman Distillery** (☏269-820-2050; www.journeymandistillery.com; 109 Generations Dr; ⊙11:30am-10pm Mon-Thu, 11:30am-11pm Fri & Sat, 10am-10pm Sun), located in the old Featherbone Factory that used to make corsets and buggy whips. Today it produces organic whiskies, gins and other booze, and serves them in its rustic bar and restaurant.

The Drive » Head north on Elm St, which becomes Three Oaks Rd. After 2.5 miles turn right onto Warren Woods Rd for six farm-flecked miles. Turn left onto Cleveland Ave for 4 miles, and then right onto Browntown Rd for 2 miles. When it ends at Hills Rd turn left. Soon you'll see Round Barn.

LINK YOUR TRIP

4 Highway 61
Ready to drive? It's 420 miles from Mackinaw City, the final stop in the Gold Coast itinerary, across the wild Northwoods of Michigan and Wisconsin to your starting point in Duluth.

❸ Round Barn Estate

By now you've noticed all the wineries signposted off the roads. Around 20 vineyards and tasting rooms cluster between New Buffalo and Saugatuck. The Lake Michigan Shore Wine Trail (www.miwinetrail. com) provides a map to several of them.

A good one to start at is **Round Barn Estate** (☏269-422-1617; www. roundbarn.com; 10983 Hills Rd, Baroda; tastings $12-20; ⏰11am-6pm Sun-Thu, to 7pm Fri & Sat May-Oct, reduced hours Nov-Apr; 🐾). It goes beyond vino with its grapes – it also uses the fruit to make DiVine Vodka. Try it in the tasting room. During the week, you're welcome to picnic on the grounds; a food truck serves snacks on weekends. Live bands play on Saturday and Sunday, and there is a $5 cover charge (it's applied to your tasting fee).

The Drive ≫ Take Hills Rd to 1st St in Baroda; turn west on Lemon Creek Rd and go to the Red Arrow Hwy (6.5 miles total). The Red Arrow becomes Lakeshore Dr as it nears St Joseph. After a few blocks as Main St it converges with Hwy 63, and in 10 miles meets the Blue Star Hwy (County Rd A-2). Follow the latter 30 miles north, then take Hwy 89 east to Fennville.

❹ Fennville

It may be a teeny farm town with a lone traffic light, but pie fanatics have been swarming here for decades. The draw: **Crane's Pie Pantry, Restaurant & Winery** (☏269-561-2297; www.cranespie pantry.com; 6054 124th Ave; pie slices $4.50; ⏰8am-7pm). Sure, you can pick your own apples and peaches in the surrounding orchards, but those in need of a quick fix beeline to the tchotchke-filled bakery for a bulging slice of flaky goodness.

Nearby **Virtue Cider** (☏269-722-3232; www. virtuecider.com; 2170 62nd St; ⏰noon-6pm Tue & Wed, to 7pm Thu-Sun) lets you sip a pint while sheep bleat, pigs oink and chickens cluck on the farm around you. The taproom is in a barrel-strewn barn, where the crisp, dry Brut is the star of the taps.

The Drive ≫ Return to the Blue Star Hwy. Drive north for 4 miles to Saugatuck.

TRIP HIGHLIGHT

❺ Saugatuck & Douglas

The strong arts community and gay-friendly vibe draw boatloads of vacationers to pretty Saugatuck. Galleries of pottery, paintings and glasswork proliferate downtown along Water and Butler Sts. Climb aboard the clackety

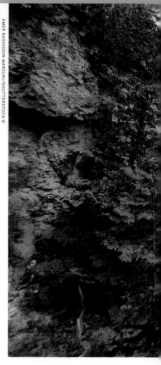

AMER RASHIDDIN MARZUKI/SHUTTERSTOCK ©

Saugatuck Chain Ferry (www.facebook.com/the saugatuckchainferry; end of Mary St; 1-way $2; ⏰9am-9pm late May-early Sep), and the operator will pull you across the Kalamazoo River. On the other side, walk to the dock's right (north) and you'll come to **Mt Baldhead**, a 764ft-high sand dune. Huff up the stairs to see the grand view, then race down the other side to beautiful **Oval Beach** (Oval Beach Dr; ⏰9am-10pm). Can't get enough sand? **Saugatuck Dune Rides** (☏269-857-2253; www.saugatuckduneride.com; 6495 Blue Star Hwy; adult/

Mackinac Island Arch Rock (p44)

child $22/12; ⊙10am-7:30pm Jul & Aug, reduced hours May, Jun, Sep & Oct, closed Nov-Apr) provides 40 minutes of fun zipping over nearby mounds.

Next door to Saugatuck is Douglas, a twin village that extends the artsy, beachy bounty.

The Drive » The Blue Star Hwy makes its slowpoke, two-lane way northeast through farmland. It becomes 58th St, then Washington Ave, then Michigan Ave and River Ave before reaching downtown Holland 12 miles later.

6 Holland

You don't have to cross the ocean for tulips, windmills and clogs. Michigan's Holland has the whole kitschy package. Take your pick of gardens and wooden-shoe factories, or better yet, seek out the city's famous suds. **New Holland Brewing** (☏616-355-6422; www.newhollandbrew.com; 66 E 8th St; ⊙11am-midnight Mon-Thu, to 1am Fri & Sat, to 10pm Sun) is known for its robust beers, such as Tangerine Space Machine and Dragon's Milk stout, all flowing in the pub.

Beach buffs can swing by **Holland State Park** (☏616-399-9390; 2215 Ottawa Beach Rd; per car $9; ⊙8am-10pm), whose strands of sand are among the state's most popular thanks to light-house views, fiery sunsets and boating action.

The Drive » At Holland State Park's northeast edge pick up Lakeshore Ave, the back-road alternative to Hwy 31. Ramble 20 miles north to Grand Haven, then filter on to Hwy 31 to speed up for 65 miles. Take exit 166 for Ludington; the park is about 10 miles north of town.

⑦ Ludington State Park

It's time to stretch the legs at **Ludington State Park** (📞231-843-2423; Hwy 116; per car $9; ☺8am-10pm). Once inside, people simply pull over on the roadside and make a break for the beautiful stretches of beach. It also has a top-notch trail system and the renovated **Big Sable Point Lighthouse** to hike to (or live in, as the volunteer lighthouse keeper). Tours of the 112ft beacon cost $5.

The Drive ›› Return to Hwy 31 and head north to Manistee. A few miles beyond town, hop on Hwy 22 toward Frankfort. The byway takes its time past inland lakes, clapboard towns and historic lighthouses as it winds to the Sleeping Bear Dunes. It's about 85 miles total.

TRIP HIGHLIGHT

⑧ Sleeping Bear Dunes National Lakeshore

Stop at the park's **visitor center** (📞231-326-4700; www.nps.gov/slbe; 9922 W Front St; ☺8:30am-6pm Jun-Aug, to 4pm Sep-May) in Empire for information, trail maps and vehicle entry permits (week/annual $25/45). Then steer north for 4 miles to the **Pierce Stocking Scenic Drive** (Hwy 109, Empire; ☺9am-sunset May–mid-Nov). The 7-mile, one-lane, picnic-grove-studded loop is one way to absorb the stunning lake vistas. Another is the **Dune Climb** (Hwy 109, Glen Arbor; ☺24hr), which entails trudging up a 200ft-high sand pile to a grand view of the azure water. There's also the **Sleeping Bear Heritage Trail** (www.sleepingbeartrail.org), which paves 22 miles from Empire north past the Dune Climb and through dreamy forested areas. Walkers and cyclists are all over it. Trailheads with parking lots are located roughly every 3 miles.

The Drive ›› After the Dune Climb, stay on Hwy 109 until it ends in bustling Glen Arbor. Rejoin Hwy 22 for 18 miles as it continues through the national lakeshore to Leland.

⑨ Leland

Little Leland couldn't be any cuter. Grab a bite at a waterfront restaurant downtown, and poke around atmospheric Fishtown with its weather-beaten fishing-shanties-cum-shops. Ferries depart from here to the forest-cloaked Manitou Islands. Day trips for hiking and beach-combing

---

↱ DETOUR: GRAND RAPIDS

Start: ⑥ Holland

The second-largest city in Michigan, Grand Rapids has gotten its groove on through beer tourism. Some 25 craft breweries operate in the city proper, and about 20 more in nearby towns. The Ale Trail takes you there (download a map at www.experiencegr.com/beer). What makes the scene so popular is the breweries' density – you can walk between many makers – and the relatively low cost of drinking. If you only have time for one stop, make it **Brewery Vivant** (📞616-719-1604; www.breweryvivant.com; 925 Cherry St SE; ☺3-11pm Mon-Thu, to midnight Fri, 11am-midnight Sat, noon-10pm Sun), which specializes in Belgian-style beers. It's set in an old chapel with stained-glass windows, a vaulted ceiling and farmhouse-style communal tables. Beer geeks adore it.

Grand Rapids lies 29 miles inland from Holland via I-196.

are doable from mid-June to early September, though rising lake levels and dock damage have halted some excursions. Check with **Manitou Island Transit** (☏231-256-9061; www.manitoutransit.com; 207 W River St; return adult/child $42/21), which also runs a sunset cruise (adult/child $25/15) along the shoreline four days per week.

The Drive ›› Take Hwy 22 north for 4 miles. Zig right on N Eagle Hwy, then left on E Kolarik Rd. A mile onward, take the first right you come to, which is Setterbo Rd. You'll spy the cider house 3.5 miles later.

- - - - - - - - - - - - - - -

⑩ Suttons Bay

On the outskirts of Suttons Bay, **Tandem Ciders** (☏231-271-0050; www.tandemciders.com; 2055 Setterbo Rd; ⊙noon-6pm Mon-Sat, to 5pm Sun) pours delicious hard ciders made from local apples in its small tasting room on the family farm. In town, **Grand Traverse Bike Tours** (☏231-421-6815; www.grandtraversebiketours.com; 318 N St Joseph St; ⊙9am-5:30pm Mon-Sat, 10am-4pm Sun) offers guided rides (four-hour tour is $89) to local wineries, as well as self-guided tours ($69 per person) for which staff provide route planning and van pickup of your wine purchases.

The Drive ›› Hwy 22 rides down the coast of Grand Traverse Bay and eventually rolls into Traverse City.

- - - - - - - - - - - - - - -

⑪ Traverse City

Michigan's 'cherry capital' is the largest city in the region. Outdoor adventures abound, and the superb food and arts scenes are comparable to those of a much larger urban area.

Front St is the main drag to wander. Pop in to **Cherry Republic** (☏231-932-9205; www.cherryrepublic.com; 154 E Front St; ⊙9am-9pm Sun-Thu, to 10pm Fri & Sat). Although touristy, it's a hoot to see all the products: cherry ketchup, cherry-dusted tortillas, cherry butter, cherry wine – you get the point. Filmmaker and local resident Michael Moore renovated the gorgeous, century-old **State Theatre** (☏231-947-3446; www.stateandbijou.org; 233 E Front St; adult/child $9/7). It shows first-run movies and art-house flicks, with 25¢ morning matinees of classics. And what's more perfect than a kayak-and-bike tour of local breweries? **Paddle TC** (☏231-492-0223; www.paddletc.com; 111 E Grandview Pkwy, Clinch Park; kayaks per hour from $30, tours from $45; ⊙9am-9pm May-Oct) makes it happen with its half-day KaBrew tour ($69, equipment included).

The Drive ›› Take Front St (Hwy 31) east out of downtown. In a half mile, turn left on Garfield Ave (Hwy 37). Follow Hwy 37 north, sallying through the grape- and cherry-planted Old Mission Peninsula.

- - - - - - - - - - - - - - -

⑫ Old Mission Peninsula

Taste-tripping through the peninsula's wineries is a popular pastime. With 10 vineyards in 19 miles, you won't go thirsty. At **Brys Estate Vineyard & Winery** (☏231-223-9303; www.brysestate.com; 3309 Blue Water Rd; ⊙11am-7pm Mon-Sat, to 6pm Sun late May-early Sep, reduced hours rest of year), cabernet franc and dry riesling are best sipped on the sprawling deck with bay views. **Chateau Chantal** (☏231-223-4110; www.chateauchantal.com; 15900 Rue de Vin; ⊙11am-8pm Mon-Sat, to 6pm Sun late May-early Sep, reduced hours rest of year) pours crowd-pleasing chardonnay and pinot noir. **Peninsula Cellars** (☏231-933-9787; www.peninsulacellars.com; 11480 Center Rd; ⊙10am-6pm Apr-Oct, to 5pm Nov-Mar), in an old schoolhouse, makes fine whites and is often less crowded.

The Drive ›› Retrace your path back to Hwy 31 in Traverse City and head north. In roughly 50 miles, north of affluent Charlevoix, look for Boyne City Rd. It skirts Lake Charlevoix and eventually arrives at the Horton Bay General Store.

⓭ Horton Bay General Store

Ernest Hemingway fans will recall the **Horton Bay General Store** (☏231-582-7827; www.hortonbaygeneral store.com; 5115 Boyne City Rd, Boyne City; ⊙10am-2pm & 5-9pm Thu-Sun, closed mid-Oct–mid-May), with its 'high false front,' from his short story 'Up in Michigan.' As a youth, Hemingway used to hang out here. His family had a cottage on nearby Walloon Lake. The retro shop now sells groceries, souvenirs and snacks, plus wine and tapas in the evening.

The Drive » Backtrack on Boyne City Rd a quarter mile to County Rd C-71 (aka Horton Bay Rd N) and turn right. Take it for 5 miles until it meets Hwy 31 north, which carries you to Petoskey in 6 miles.

⓮ Petoskey

A vintage resort town jammed with yachts, foodie cafes and gastropubs, Petoskey also features a couple of Hemingway sights. The **Little Traverse Historical Museum** (☏231-347-2620; www.petoskeymuseum.org; 100 Depot Ct; adult/child $3/free; ⊙10am-4pm Mon-Sat Jun-Oct) has a collection dedicated to the author, including rare first-edition books that Hemingway autographed for a friend when he visited in 1947. Afterward, toss back a drink at **City Park Grill** (☏231-347-0101; www.cityparkgrill.com; 432 E Lake St; ⊙11:30am-10pm Sun-Thu, to 1:30am Fri & Sat), where Hemingway was a regular. Just north of town you can hunt for famed Petoskey stones (honeycomb-patterned fragments of ancient coral) at **Petoskey State Park** (☏231-347-2311; 2475 Hwy 119, Petoskey; per car $9).

The Drive » Time for a choice: take the 'fast' way to Mackinaw City via Hwy 31 (a 45-minute drive), or dawdle on narrow Hwy 119 (a 90-minute drive). The latter curves through thick forest as part of the Tunnel of Trees scenic route. It ends in Cross Village, where Levering Rd takes you east to rejoin Hwy 31.

TRIP HIGHLIGHT

⓯ Mackinac Island

Mackinaw City is the jumping-off point to Mackinac Island, a petite charmer speckled with Victorian cottages and 18th-century fortresses. Cars are banned, and all travel is by horse or bicycle, adding to the old-time mood. Highlights include **Fort Mackinac** (☏906-847-3328; www.mackinacparks.com; 7127 Huron Rd; adult/child $13.50/8; ⊙9:30am-7pm Jun-Aug, reduced hours May & Sep–mid-Oct, closed mid-Oct–Apr; 🚸), built in 1780 and known for its views and costumed interpreters who fire cannons; and **Arch Rock**, which curves 150ft above the lake and provides dramatic photo ops. You can cycle around the island in an hour. Bike rentals ($10 per hour) are ubiquitous.

Two ferry companies – **Shepler's** (☏800-828-6157; www.sheplersferry.com; 556 E Central Ave; return adult/child/bicycle $27/16/13; ⊙late Apr-Oct) and **Star Line** (☏800-638-9892; www.mack-inacferry.com; 801 S Huron Ave; return adult/child/bicycle $27/16/13) – have docks in Mackinaw City and make frequent trips. The ride takes 20 minutes, so it's easy to do as a day trip.

➡ DETOUR: BEAVER ISLAND

Start: ⓭ **Horton Bay**

For an alternative to Mackinac Island, sail to quieter Beaver Island (www.beaverisland.org), an Irish-influenced enclave of some 600 people that offers hiking, biking, and kayaking, and snorkeling to shipwrecked schooners. The **ferry** (☏231-547-2311; www.bibco.com; 103 Bridge Park Dr, Charlevoix; 1-way adult/child/car $32.50/20/105; ⊙mid-Apr–late Dec) departs from downtown Charlevoix. The trip takes two hours.

Right Horton Bay General Store

Highway 61

Waterfalls, moose and Bob Dylan vestiges roll by on Minnesota's Hwy 61. The road grips Lake Superior's shore, tucked between red-tinged cliffs and towering firs from Duluth to Canada's edge.

4

TRIP HIGHLIGHTS

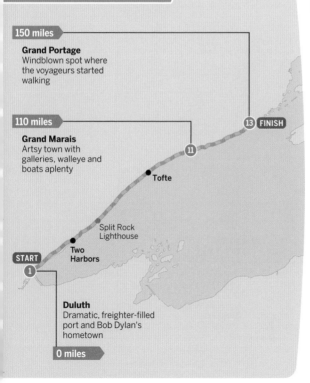

150 miles

Grand Portage
Windblown spot where the voyageurs started walking

110 miles

Grand Marais
Artsy town with galleries, walleye and boats aplenty

Tofte

Split Rock Lighthouse

Two Harbors

START **1**

Duluth
Dramatic, freighter-filled port and Bob Dylan's hometown

0 miles

13 FINISH

11

**2–3 DAYS
150 MILES / 241KM**

GREAT FOR...

BEST TIME TO GO

July to mid-October for pleasant weather and fall colors.

ESSENTIAL PHOTO

Split Rock Lighthouse on its perfect clifftop.

BEST FOR WILDLIFE

Drive the Gunflint Trail and watch for moose.

---

4 Highway 61

Mention Hwy 61 and many folks hum Bob Dylan. But this North Shore road is not about murder, poverty or any other mean-street mumblings from his 1965 album 'Highway 61 Revisited'. Instead it's a journey dominated by water, where ore-toting freighters ply the ports, little fishing fleets haul in the day's catch, and wave-bashed cliffs offer Superior views if you're willing to trek.

TRIP HIGHLIGHT

1 Duluth

Duluth is a brawny shot-and-a-beer port town that immerses visitors in its storied history as a major shipping center. Start downtown at the **Aerial Lift Bridge**, Duluth's landmark that raises its mighty arm to let horn-bellowing freighters into the harbor. About 1000 vessels per year glide through. The screens inside the **Maritime Visitor Center** (📞218-720-5260; www.

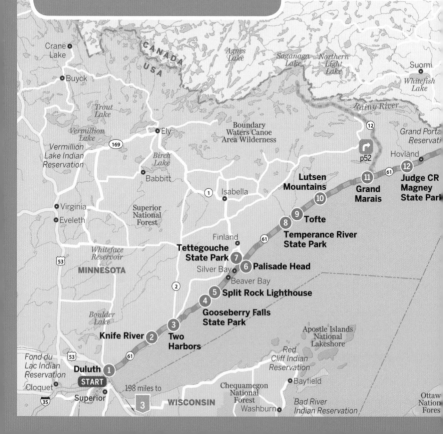

lsmma.com; 600 Canal Park Dr; ☺10am-9pm Jun-Aug, reduced hours Sep-May) tell what time the behemoths come and go. Cool model boats and exhibits on Great Lakes shipwrecks add to the museum's top marks.

Duluth is also the birthplace of Bob Dylan, though the town is pretty laid-back about its famous son. **Dylan's first home** (519 N 3rd Ave E) lies up a hill a few blocks northeast of downtown. He lived on the upper floor until age six, when his family moved inland to Hibbing. A small plaque over the front porch marks the spot.

For a hip scene of indie breweries, cider makers and restaurants, ramble through the Lincoln Park Craft District, west of downtown.

The Drive » Take London Rd, aka Hwy 61, heading northeast out of town. Follow the signs for the North Shore Scenic Dr (also called Scenic 61 or Old Hwy 61). There's a Hwy 61 expressway that also covers the next 20 miles, but steer clear and dawdle on the original, curvy, two-lane route instead.

---

② Knife River

Unspoiled shoreline and fisherfolk casting at river mouths are your companions along the way until you reach **Russ Kendall's Smoke House** (☎218-834-5995; www.facebook.com/russkendalls; 149 Scenic Dr; ☺9:30am-5:30pm) in Knife River. A groovy neon sign beckons you in. Four generations of Kendall folk have cooked up the locally plucked trout and line-caught Alaskan salmon. Buy a brown-sugar-cured slab, staff will wrap it in newspaper, and you'll be set for picnics for miles to come.

The Drive » Continue northeast on Hwy 61 through the pines. In about 9 miles you'll reach Two Harbors.

---

③ Two Harbors

Industry prevails in Two Harbors, the biggest town you'll encounter for the rest of the route. Watch iron-ore freighters maneuvering around the huge docks that jut into Agate Bay, and check out Minnesota's only operating **lighthouse** (www.lakecounty historicalsociety.org; $5; ☺10am-6pm Mon-Sat, to 4pm Sun), an 1892 redbrick fog-buster that doubles as a B&B. In case you're wondering: the other harbor that gives the town its name is Burlington Bay, around the point to the north.

Hikers should stop at the **Superior Hiking Trail Office** (☎218-834-2700; www.superiorhiking.org; 731 7th Ave, Suite 2; ☺10am-4:30pm Mon, Thu & Fri) for information on the pristine, 300-mile footpath that follows the ridgeline above Lake Superior between Duluth and the Canadian border. Trailheads with parking lots pop up every 5 to 10 miles, making it ideal for day hikes. Overnight hikers will find 94 backcountry campsites and several lodges along the way.

The Drive » Motor onward on Hwy 61, past the hamlet of Castle Danger (named for a boat that ran aground nearby) to Gooseberry Falls State Park, a 13-mile drive.

Thunder Bay

Kakabeka Falls

Grand Portage

③ **FINISH**

p54

Isle Royale National Park

Lake Superior

Ontonagon Indian Reservation

Ontonagon

MICHIGAN

Ⓝ 0 ——————— 40 km
0 ——————— 20 miles

④ Gooseberry Falls State Park

The five cascades, scenic gorge and easy trails draw carloads of visitors to **Gooseberry Falls State Park** (☎218-834-3855; www.dnr.state.mn.us; 3206 Hwy 61; per car $7; ⏰8am-10pm; ♿). Several smart stone and log buildings, built by Civilian Conservation Corps in the 1930s, dot the premises and hold exhibits and concessions.

The **Lower and Middle Falls** offer the quickest access via a 0.6-mile paved walkway. Hardier types can trek the 2-mile **Gooseberry River Loop**, which is part of the Superior Hiking Trail. To embark, leave your car at the visitor center lot (at Mile Post 38.9). Follow the trail to the Upper Falls, then continue upstream on the Fifth Falls Trail. Cross the bridge at Fifth Falls, then return on the river's other side to where you started. Voila! It's one of the simplest Superior trail jaunts you'll find.

The Drive » Yep, it's back to Hwy 61 heading northeast, this time for 7 miles.

⑤ Split Rock Lighthouse

Split Rock Lighthouse State Park (☎218-595-7625; www.dnr.state.mn.us; 3755 Split Rock Lighthouse Rd, Two Harbors; per car $7, lighthouse $8; ⏰by reservation 10am-6pm mid-May–mid-Oct, 11am-4pm Thu-Mon mid-Oct–mid-May) is the most visited spot on the entire North Shore. The shiner itself is a state historic site with a separate admission fee to the grounds. If you don't mind stairs, say 170 or so each way, tramp down the cliff to the beach for incredible views of the lighthouse and surrounding shore.

The lighthouse was built after a whopping storm in November 1905 battered 29 ships in the area. Modern navigation equipment rendered it obsolete by 1969. No matter. It remains one of the most picture-perfect structures you'll come across.

SCRUGGELGREEN/SHUTTERSTOCK ©

The Drive » Onward on Hwy 61 for 10 miles. Not long after cruising by the factory town of Silver Bay, watch for the sign to Palisade Head.

⑥ Palisade Head

Palisade Head is an old lava flow that morphed into some awesomely sheer, rust-red cliffs. A narrow road winds around to the top, where there's a small parking lot. The view that unfurls is tremendous. On a clear day you can see Wisconsin's Apostle Islands. Rock climbers love the Head, and you'll

---

HWY 61'S OTHER INCARNATION

Hwy 61 is also used to reference the fabled Blues Hwy that tracks the Mississippi River en route to New Orleans. That road is actually US 61, and it starts near St Paul, MN. Our Hwy 61 is the state scenic road that starts in Duluth.

Duluth Aerial Lift Bridge (p48)

probably see a lot of them hanging around.

The Drive » Return to Hwy 61. Palisade Head is actually part of Tettegouche State Park, though it's not contiguous. The park's main span begins 2 miles up the road.

7 Tettegouche State Park

Like most of the parks dotting the North Shore, **Tettegouche State Park** (☏218-353-8800; www.dnr. state.mn.us; 5702 Hwy 61; per car $7; ☻8am-10pm) offers fishing, camping, paddling and hiking trails to waterfalls and little lakes, plus skiing and snowshoe trails in winter.

There are two unique to-dos, both accessed near the park entrance (Mile 58.5). Leave your car in the parking lot by the visitor center, then hit the trail to **Shovel Point**. It's a 1.5-mile round-trip jaunt over lots of steps and boardwalks. It pays off with sublime views of the rugged landscape from the point's tip. Watch the lake's awesome power as waves smash below. And keep an eye out for peregrine falcons that nest in the

area. Tettegouche's other cool feature is the idyllic **swimming hole** at the Baptism River's mouth. Walk along the picnic area by the visitor center and you'll run into it.

The Drive » Hwy 61 rolls by more birch trees, parks and cloud-flecked skies for the next 22 miles. Not far past Taconite Harbor and its shuttered power plant, you'll come to Temperance River.

8 Temperance River State Park

Get ready for another gorgeous, falls-filled landscape. The

51

eponymous waterway at **Temperance River State Park** (📞218-663-3100; www.dnr.state.mn.us; 7620 Hwy 61, Tofte; per car $7; ⏱8am-10pm) belies its moderate name and roars through a narrow, twisting gorge. The scene is easy to get to, with highway-side parking. Then hike over footbridges and around rock pools to see the action.

The Drive » It's a quick 2 miles up Hwy 61 to Tofte.

9 Tofte

The teeny town of Tofte is worth a stop to browse the **North Shore Commercial Fishing Museum** (📞218-663-7050; www.commercialfishingmuseum.org; 7136 Hwy 61, Tofte; adult/child $3/1; ⏱9am-3pm Tue-Thu, to 5pm Fri & Sat mid-May–mid-Oct, 10am-5pm Fri & Sat mid-Oct–mid-May).

The twin-gabled red building holds fishing nets, a fishing boat and other tools of the trade, as well as intriguing photos, most of them from the original Norwegian families who settled and fished here in the late 1800s.

Nearby **Sawtooth Outfitters** (📞218-663-7643; www.sawtoothoutfitters.com; 7213 Hwy 61, Tofte; ⏱8am-6pm daily May-late Oct & mid-late Dec, 8am-6pm Thu-Mon Jan-early Apr) offers guided kayaking tours (half-/full-day tours $65/120) for all levels of paddling. It has trips on the Temperance River and out on Lake Superior, as well as easier jaunts on wildlife-rich inland lakes. Sawtooth also rents mountain bikes (per day from $24) to pedal over the many trails in the area, including the popular **Gitchi Gami State Bike Trail** (www.ggta.org).

The Drive » Get back on Hwy 61 and head 7 piney miles northeast. Turn left on Ski Hill Rd.

10 Lutsen Mountains

Lutsen (📞218-663-7281; www.lutsen.com; 467 Ski Hill Rd; lift ticket per day adult/child $92/72; ⏱10am-5pm May-Oct, 9am-4pm Nov-Apr) is a ski resort – the biggest alpine ski area in the Midwest, in fact. So it bustles in winter when skiers and snowboarders pile in for the 95 runs on four mountains.

In summer, visitors come for the scenic **aerial gondola** (round-trip adult/child $25/17) to the top of Moose Mountain. The cars glide at treetop level into the valley and over

---

DETOUR: GUNFLINT TRAIL

Start: 11 Grand Marais

The Gunflint Trail, aka County Rd 12, slices inland from Grand Marais to Saganaga Lake. The paved, 57-mile-long byway dips into the Boundary Waters Canoe Area Wilderness (www.fs.usda.gov/attmain/superior/specialplaces), the legendarily remote paddlers' paradise. The **Gunflint Ranger Station** (📞218-387-1750; 2020 Hwy 61; ⏱8am-4:30pm, closed Sat & Sun Oct-Apr), just southwest of Grand Marais, has permits and information.

Even if you're not canoeing, the road presents exceptional hiking, picnicking and moose-viewing opportunities. It takes 1½ hours to drive one way, but you'll want longer to commune with your new antlered friends. There aren't any towns along the route, but several lodges are tucked in the woods where you can grab a meal or snack.

the Poplar River before reaching the mountain top 1000ft later.

Gape at the view from the chalet and hike the paths. The Superior Hiking Trail cuts through and you can take it plus a spur for the 4.5-mile trek back down the mountain.

Kids go crazy for the **alpine slide** (per person $14) on Eagle Mountain; it's accessed by chairlift. The resort also arranges family-friendly canoe trips in voyageur-style vessels (per person $15; times vary) on the Poplar River.

The Drive » Back to Hwy 61, past maple- and birch-rich Cascade River State Park (particularly lovely in fall), for 20 miles to Grand Marais.

TRIP HIGHLIGHT

⑪ Grand Marais

Home to an art colony since 1947, pretty Grand Marais makes an excellent base to explore the region. Stroll the waterfront and take advantage of the downtown filled with bars, restaurants, galleries and antique shops. Do-it-yourself enthusiasts can learn to build boats, tie flies or harvest wild rice at the **North House Folk School** (☎218-387-9762; www.northhouse.org; 500 W Hwy 61). The course list is phenomenal – including a day-long class on sailing aboard the Viking

Judge CR Magney State Park

schooner *Hjordis* (per person $150). Reserve in advance.

The Drive » On Hwy 61 beyond Grand Marais, the traffic thins and the lake reveals itself more. After 14 miles, you'll arrive at Judge CR Magney State Park.

----

⑫ Judge CR Magney State Park

Magney State Park (☎218-387-6300; www.dnr.state.mn.us; 4051 Hwy 61; per car $7; ◷8am-10pm) – named after the Minnesota Supreme Court justice who helped preserve the area – is a beauty. See it by hiking to **Devil's Kettle**, the famous falls where the Brule River splits around a huge rock. Half of the flow drops 50ft in a typically gorgeous North Shore gush, but the other half disappears down a hole and flows under-

ground. Where it goes is a mystery – scientists have never been able to determine the water's outlet. It's a moderately breath-sapping 1.1-mile walk each way.

A short distance beyond the park entrance is **Naniboujou Lodge** (☎218-387-2688; www.naniboujou.com; 20 Naniboujou Trail; r $130-180; ◷late May-late Oct; P ❄ 🛜). The 1920s property was once a private club for Babe Ruth and his contemporaries. You're welcome to walk in and look at the Great Hall (now the lodge's dining room), where mind-blowing, psychedelic-colored Cree Indian designs are painted on the domed ceiling.

The Drive » For the next 20 miles trees and rivers flash by, and Hwy 61 passes through the Grand Portage Reservation.

DETOUR:
ISLE ROYALE NATIONAL PARK

Start: ⑬ **Grand Portage**

Isle Royale National Park (www.nps.gov/isro) is technically part of Michigan, but it's easily accessed from Grand Portage. **Ferries** (☎218-600-0765; www.isleroyaleboats.com; Upper Rd; day trip adult/child $76/70) sail to the park in Lake Superior three to five days per week. The 210-sq-mile island is totally free of vehicles and roads, and gets fewer visitors in a year than Yellowstone National Park gets in a day. Wilderness buffs love it for backcountry hiking, moose spotting, camping and kayaking.

Day trips leave Grand Portage in the morning, travel for 90 minutes to get to the island, spend four hours there, then return by 3:30pm. They operate mid-June to early September. Other ferries take passengers with gear who plan to stay longer. They operate mid-May to early October.

Turn right on County Rd 17 (Mile Creek Rd) near the Trading Post.

- - - - - - - - - - - - - - - - - - -

TRIP HIGHLIGHT

⑬ Grand Portage

Grand Portage National Monument (☎218-475-0123; www.nps.gov/grpo; 170 Mile Creek Rd; ⏰10am-5pm Jun–mid-Oct) is where the early voyagers had to carry their canoes around the Pigeon River rapids. It was the center of a far-flung fur-trading empire, and the reconstructed 1788 trading post and Ojibwe village show how the little community lived in the harsh environment. Learn how the original inhabitants prepared wild rice and pressed beaver pelts as you wander through the Great Hall, kitchen, canoe warehouse and other buildings with costumed interpreters.

The half-mile paved path that goes to Mount Rose rewards with killer views. Or make like a voyageur and walk the 17-mile round-trip Grand Portage Trail that traces the early fur men's route.

Grand Portage is impressively lonely and windblown – fitting for the end of the road. Because with that, Hwy 61 concludes at the Canadian border 6 miles later.

Right Grand Portage

Destinations

Midwest & the Great Lakes (p58)

Amid the endless horizons you'll find cosmopolitan oases, surfing beaches, resort towns and moose-filled national parks.

Midwest & the Great Lakes

In this vast and underappreciated region you'll find cosmopolitan cities like Chicago and Kansas City, alpine wonders in the Black Hills, and soaring bluffs along the Mississippi and Missouri Rivers.

There are also illuminating tales of comings and goings, from Okies fleeing the Dust Bowl along Route 66 to Lewis and Clark navigating the American frontier and the Five Civilized Tribes marching westward on a Trail of Tears.

And then there are the Great Lakes. Don't be fooled by all the corn. Behind it lurks surfing beaches and Tibetan temples, car-free islands and the green-draped night lights of the aurora borealis. The Great Lakes takes its knocks for being middle-of-nowhere boring, so consider the moose-filled national parks and Hemingway, Dylan and Vonnegut sites to be its little secret.

The Great Lakes themselves are huge, like inland seas, offering beaches, dunes, resort towns and lighthouse-dotted scenery. Dairy farms and fruit orchards blanket the region, meaning fresh pie and ice cream aplenty. And when the scenery does flatten out? There's always a goofball roadside attraction to revive imaginations.

Great distances across these beguiling wide-open spaces are the biggest impediment to enjoying this enormous region.

Many sights lie near the interstates, but many more are found along the ever-intriguing small roads – the 'blue highways' of lore.

MISSOURI

The most populated state in the Plains, Missouri likes to mix things up, serving visitors ample portions of both sophisticated city life and down-home country sights. St Louis and Kansas City are the region's most interesting cities, and each is a destination in its own right. But, with more forest and less farm field than neighboring states, Missouri also cradles plenty of wild places and wide-open spaces, most notably the rolling Ozark Mountains, where the winding valleys invite adventurous exploration or just some laid-back meandering behind the steering wheel. Maybe you'll find an adventure worthy of Hannibal native Mark Twain as you wander the state.

ℹ Information

Missouri Division of Tourism (www.visitmo. com)

Bed & Breakfast Inns of Missouri (www.bbim. org)

Missouri State Parks (www.mostateparks. com) State parks are free to visit.

St Louis

POP 318,100

Revel in the unique vibe of the largest city in the Great Plains. Beer, bowling and baseball are some of the top attractions, but history and culture, much of it linked to the Mississippi River, are a vital part of the fabric. And, of course, there's the iconic Gateway Arch that you have seen in a million pictures; it's even more impressive in reality. Many music legends, including Scott Joplin, Chuck Berry, Tina Turner and Miles Davis, got their start here and jammin' live-music venues keep the flame burning.

This old city by the river is a sensational place for food and nightlife. Plan on adding an extra day or more to your trip, for time to explore.

◉ Sights

★ Gateway Arch
National Park   NATIONAL PARK

(📞877-982-1410; www.gatewayarch.com; 11 N 4th St; tram ride adult/child from $12/8; ⊙grounds 5am-11pm, Arch by reservation 8am-10pm Jun-Aug, 9am-6pm Sep-May, last tram 1hr before closing; ♿) As a symbol for St Louis, the Gateway Arch has soared above any expectations its backers could have had in 1965 when it opened. Now the centerpiece of its own recently christened national park, the silvery, shimmering Arch is the Great Plains' own Eiffel Tower. It stands 630ft high and symbolizes St Louis' historical role as 'Gateway to the West.' It's the design of the legendary Finnish American architect Eero Saarinen (1910–61).

The tram ride takes you to the tight confines at the top. Book tickets in advance online or by phone. At busy times, same-day tickets may be sold out. At the base, there is the interesting Museum at the Gateway Arch (p28). You can also buy tickets for a documentary *Monument to the Dream* (adult/child $7/3). Various money-saving combo tickets are available; some include rides on the Gateway Arch Riverboats (p60).

A massive project transformed the area around the Arch in time for its 50th birthday. The large Luther Ely Smith Square now covers noxious I-44 and connects the Arch and its park directly to the Old Courthouse and the rest of Downtown. It's a huge and welcome improvement.

A pro tip: the parkland around the Arch is a great place to escape the crowds and relax with a view of the Mississippi River.

★ City Museum   MUSEUM

(www.citymuseum.org; 701 N 15th St; $16, with rooftop $21; ⊙9am-5pm Mon-Thu, to midnight Fri & Sat, 11am-5pm Sun; ♿) Possibly the wildest highlight of any visit to St Louis is this frivolous, frilly fun house in a vast old shoe factory. The Museum of Mirth, Mystery & Mayhem sets the tone. Run, jump and explore all manner of exhibits, including a seven-story slide. The summer-only rooftop offers all manner of weird and wonderful fun, including a flamboyant Ferris wheel and a wild slide.

National Blues Museum   MUSEUM

(📞314-925-0016; www.nationalbluesmuseum. org; 615 Washington Ave; adult/child $15/10; ⊙10am-5pm Tue-Thu & Sat, to 9pm Fri, noon-5pm Sun & Mon) This flashy museum explores

ST LOUIS NEIGHBORHOODS

The St Louis neighborhoods of most interest radiate out from the Downtown core:

Central West End Just east of Forest Park, a posh center for nightlife and shopping.

Grand Center Located in Midtown and rich with cultural attractions, theaters and historic sites.

The Hill An Italian American neighborhood with good delis and restaurants.

Lafayette Square Historic, upscale and trendy.

The Loop Northwest of Forest Park; funky shops and nightlife line Delmar Blvd.

Soulard The city's oldest quarter, with good cafes, bars and blues.

South Grand Bohemian and gentrifying; surrounds beautiful Tower Grove Park and has a slew of ethnic restaurants.

Downtown St Louis

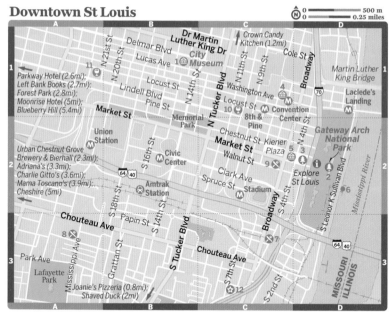

Downtown St Louis

blues legends like hometown hero Chuck Berry, while making a strong case for the genre's myriad influences on modern rock, folk, R&B and more. There are interactive exhibits from the likes of Jack White, and interesting stories about the early years of blues and its (almost exclusively female) pioneers.

Anheuser-Busch Brewery BREWERY
(☑314-577-2626; www.budweisertours.com; cnr 12th & Lynch Sts; ⊙10am-5pm Mar-Oct, 11am-4:30pm Nov-Feb) **FREE** One of the world's largest beer plants, the historic Anheuser-Busch Brewery gives marketing-driven tours. View the bottling plant and Clydesdale horses. One thing to

note: the purchase of this St Louis (and American) icon by Belgium's InBev in 2008 is still a sore spot locally. And don't ask: 'How do you remove all the flavor?'

✦ Festivals & Events

Big Muddy Blues Festival MUSIC
(www.bigmuddybluesfestival.com; Laclede's Landing; ⊙early Sep) Three stages of riverfront blues at Laclede's Landing on the Labor Day weekend.

☞ Tours

Gateway Arch Riverboats BOATING
(☑877-982-1410; www.gatewayarch.com; 50 S Leonor K Sullivan Blvd; 1hr tour adult/child from $19/8; ⊙Mar-Nov) Churn up the Big Mud-

dy on replica 19th-century steamboats. A park ranger narrates the midday cruises in season, and those after 3pm sail subject to availability. There are also numerous dinner and drinking cruises. Various combo tickets are available with attractions at the Gateway Arch National Park (p59).

🛏 Sleeping

⭐Cheshire   HOTEL $$
(📞314-647-7300; www.cheshirestl.com; 6300 Clayton Rd; r $145-250; 🅿❄🛜🏊) This up-scale inn near **Forest Park** (📞314-367-7275; www.forestparkforever.org; bounded by Lindell Blvd, Kingshighway Blvd & I-64; ⏱6am-10pm; 🚗) **FREE** oozes character, from its stained-glass windows to the all-encompassing British literary theme. The hodgepodge of artworks, antique furnishings and (occasionally frightening) taxidermy are sure to delight.

Parkway Hotel   HOTEL $$
(📞314-256-7777; www.theparkwayhotel.com; 4550 Forest Park Ave; r $160-250; 🅿❄@🛜) Right in the midst of Central West End's upscale fun, this indie eight-story hotel contains 217 remodeled rooms (with refrigerators and microwaves) inside a grand limestone building. A hot buffet breakfast is included, and you can't beat the location right across from Forest Park. The decor is sleek and contemporary.

Moonrise Hotel   BOUTIQUE HOTEL $$
(📞314-721-1111; www.moonrisehotel.com; 6177 Delmar Blvd; r $155-450; 🅿❄🛜🏊) The stylish eight-story Moonrise has a high profile amid the high energy of the Loop neighborhood. Its 125 rooms sport a lunar motif, but are grounded enough to slow things down to comfy.

✕ Eating

⭐Adriana's   ITALIAN $
(📞314-773-3833; www.adrianasonthehill.com; 5101 Shaw Ave, The Hill; mains $5-10; ⏱10:30am-3pm Mon-Sat) Redolent of herbs, this family-owned Italian deli serves up fresh salads and sandwiches (get the meaty Hill Boy) to ravenous lunching crowds. The thin-crust pizza is also a treat; ask about the off-the-menu specials. Expect lines.

Crown Candy Kitchen   CAFE $
(📞314-621-9650; www.crowncandykitchen.net; 1401 St Louis Ave; mains $5-10; ⏱10:30am-8pm Mon-Thu, to 9pm Fri & Sat; 🚗) An authentic family-run soda fountain that's been mak-

ing families smile since 1913. Malts (hot fudge, yum!) come with spoons, the floats, well, float, and you can try the famous BLT. Homemade candies top it off.

⭐Broadway Oyster Bar   CAJUN $$
(📞314-621-8811; www.broadwayoysterbar.com; 736 S Broadway; mains $10-20; ⏱11am-3am) Part bar, part live-music venue, but all restaurant, this joint jumps year-round. When the sun shines, people flock outside where they suck down crawfish and other Cajun treats. It's nuts before and after Cardinals games.

Shaved Duck   AMERICAN $$
(📞314-776-1407; www.theshavedduck.com; 2900 Virginia Ave; mains $10-23; ⏱11am-9pm Mon, to 10pm Tue-Sat, noon-8pm Sun) A South Grand stalwart, the Shaved Duck fires up its grills early in the day and turns out excellent BBQ, such as the signature smoked duck. Options include fab sandwiches and veggie sides. Live music weeknights.

Eleven Eleven Mississippi   TUSCAN $$
(📞314-241-9999; www.1111-m.com; 1111 Mississippi Ave; mains $9-25; ⏱11am-10pm Mon-Thu, to 11pm Fri, 5-11pm Sat; 🚗) This popular bistro and wine bar fills an old shoe factory. Dinner mains have a Tuscan flair and farm-to-table vibe. Other options on the seasonal menu include sandwiches, pizzas, steaks and veggie dishes. Excellent wine selection.

DRINK LOCAL

Schlafly (📞314-241-2337; www.schlafly.com; 2100 Locust St; ⏱11am-10pm Mon-Thu, to midnight Fri & Sat, noon-9pm Sun), **Civic Life** (www.thecivillife.com; 3714 Holt Ave; ⏱4-11pm Tue-Thu, noon-11pm Fri & Sat, 11am-9pm Sun), **Earthbound Brewing** (📞314-769-9576; www.earthboundbeer.com; 2724 Cherokee St; ⏱4pm-midnight Tue-Fri, from noon Sat, noon-10pm Sun) and **Urban Chestnut** (📞314-222-0143; www.urbanchestnut.com; 4465 Manchester Ave; ⏱11am-11pm Mon-Thu, to 1am Fri & Sat, to 9pm Sun) are excellent local microbrews that will let you forget that you're in the home of Bud. The website STL Hops (www.stlhops.com) is an excellent guide to local beers and where to drink them.

STRETCH YOUR LEGS
ST LOUIS

Start/Finish: Forest Park Visitor & Education Center

Distance: 4 miles

Duration: 3 hours

The Gateway Arch downtown is an obvious drawcard, but for real walking pleasure, join the masses in leafy, museum- and attraction-filled Forest Park. The Central West End neighborhood to the east adds to the fun.

Take this walk on Trip

2

Forest Park

New York City may have Central Park, but St Louis has bigger Forest Park (bounded by Lindell Blvd, Kingshighway Blvd & I-64; ⊗6am-10pm; 🚻). The superb, 1371-acre spread was the setting of the 1904 World's Fair. The Visitor & Education Center (☑314-367-7275; www.forestparkforever.org; 5595 Grand Dr; ⊗6am-5pm; ☎) is in an old streetcar pavilion and has a cafe. Park your car here and start your walk.

The Walk ≫ Walk northwest through the well-tended grounds some 300m.

Missouri History Museum

The museum (☑314-746-4599; www.mo-history.org; 5700 Lindell Blvd; ⊗by reservation 10am-5pm Wed-Mon, to 8pm Tue; 🅿) presents the story of St Louis, starring the World's Fair, a replica of Charles Lindbergh's plane and a host of bluesmen. Oral histories from those who fought segregation are moving.

The Walk ≫ Walk south past the tennis courts to the lake's small marina.

Post-Dispatch Lake

Still showing signs of its central position during the World's Fair, this large lake isn't just for ogling: rent a boat from the Boathouse (☑314-722-6872; www.boathousestl.com; 6101 Government Dr, Forest Park; boat rental per hour from $15; ⊗11am-approx 1hr before sunset Tue-Sun, weather permitting) and explore the placid waters.

The Walk ≫ Walk southwest to the art museum, or take the prettier sinuous path along the north side of the lakes, then drop down south past the Grand Basin and across the grassy expanse of Art Hill.

St Louis Art Museum

A grand beaux-arts palace originally built for the World's Fair, it now houses the storied St Louis Art Museum (www.slam.org; 1 Fine Arts Dr; ⊗10am-5pm Tue-Thu, Sat & Sun, to 9pm Fri), which has a collection that spans time and styles.

The Walk ≫ A short verdant stroll southeast and you are at the north entrance to the zoo.

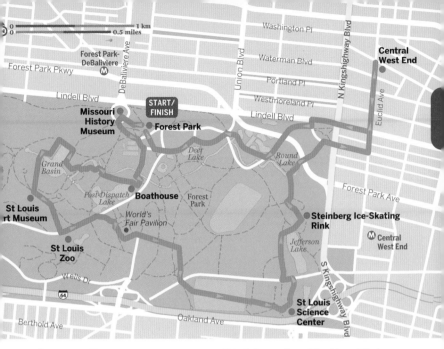

St Louis Zoo

A world-class facility, the vast zoo (☎314-781-0900; www.stlzoo.org; 1 Government Dr; fee for some exhibits; ⊙by reservation 9am-5pm daily, to 7pm Fri-Sun May-Sep; P ♿) includes a fascinating River's Edge area with African critters.

The Walk ⟫ Walk straight east through the tree-shaded grounds, watching for the planetarium in the distance. You might pause at the beautiful 1909 World's Fair Pavilion, a grand open-air shelter built with proceeds from the 1904 fair.

St Louis Science Center

Live demonstrations, dinosaurs, a planetarium and an IMAX theater are just some of the highlights of the St Louis Science Center (☎314-289-4400; www.slsc.org; 5050 Oakland Ave; ⊙by reservation 9:30am-5:30pm Mon-Sat, from 11am Sun; P ♿), much of which is reached via a dramatic glass walkway over I-64.

The Walk ⟫ Follow the wide main pedestrian path north past Jefferson Lake.

Steinberg Ice-Skating Rink

If it's too cold to rent a boat, it's probably just right to go ice-skating with lots of other happy skaters at the Steinberg Skating Rink (☎314-367-7465; www.steinbergrink.com; 400 Jefferson Dr; admission $8, skate rental $7; ⊙10am-9pm Sun-Thu, to 11pm Fri & Sat mid-Nov–Feb).

The Walk ⟫ Leave the park, crossing S Kingshighway Blvd, and walk one block to Euclid Ave, the heart of the Central West End area.

Central West End

This posh center for cafes and shopping is anchored by Euclid Ave. Get a picnic lunch at top-notch Pickles Deli (☎314-361-3354; www.facebook.com/picklesdelistl; 22 N Euclid Ave; mains $6-10; ⊙9am-3pm Mon-Fri, from 10am Sat; ♿). Nearby is Left Bank Books (☎314-367-6731; www.left-bank.com; 399 N Euclid Ave; ⊙10am-10pm Mon-Sat, 11am-6pm Sun), a great indie bookstore.

The Walk ⟫ Return to the car park via some of the nicest gardens in Forest Park. Follow the paths along the waterways linking Round and Deer Lakes.

🍷 Drinking & Nightlife

Laclede's Landing, Soulard and the Loop are loaded with pubs and bars, many with live music. Most bars close at 1:30am, though some have 3am licenses.

The Grove, a strip of Manchester Ave between Kingshighway Blvd and S Vandeventer Ave, is the hub of St Louis' LGBTIQ+ community. Peruse *Vital Voice* (www.the vitalvoice.com) for info.

★**Blueberry Hill**   BAR
(☑314-727-4444; www.blueberryhill.com; 6504 Delmar Blvd; ☺11am-late) St Louis native Chuck Berry rocked the small basement bar here until the day he died in 2017. The venue hosts bands big and small and has good pub food (mains $7 to $15), arcade games, darts and walls covered in pop-culture memorabilia.

Bridge Tap House & Wine Bar   BAR
(☑314-241-8141; www.thebridgestl.com; 1004 Locust St; ☺4-11pm) Slip onto a sofa or rest your elbows on a table at this romantic bar where you can savor fine wine or the best local beer (over 50 on tap) and nibble a variety of exquisite little bites from a seasonal menu.

☆ Entertainment

★**Venice Cafe**   BLUES, JAZZ
(☑314-772-5994; www.thevenicecafe.com; 1903 Pestalozzi St; ☺4pm-1am Mon-Sat) A true cabinet of curiosities. The interior of this two-level club is a master class in mosaics, while the rambling outdoor garden is chock-full of folk art and twinkling lights. Best of all, the drinks are cheap and there's live blues, rock and jazz seven days a week.

Old Rock House   LIVE MUSIC
(☑314-534-1111; www.oldrockhouse.com; 1200 S 7th St) A great, sweaty club that draws big regional acts. Look for rock (new *and* old), blues, country, punk, metal and more.

🛍 Shopping

★**Left Bank Books**   BOOKS
(☑314-367-6731; www.left-bank.com; 399 N Euclid Ave; ☺10am-10pm Mon-Sat, 11am-6pm Sun) A great indie bookstore stocking new and used titles. There are recommendations of books by local authors and frequent author readings.

ⓘ Information

Explore St Louis (☑314-421-1023; www.explorestlouis.com; Gateway Arch Visitor Center, Luther Ely Smith Square, West entrance; ☺9am-5pm; 🖥) An excellent resource, with another branch at the airport.

Forest Park Visitor & Education Center (☑314-367-7275; www.forestparkforever.org; 5595 Grand Dr; ☺6am-5pm; 🖥) Located in an old streetcar pavilion and has a cafe. Free walking tours leave from here, or you can borrow an audio tour.

MIDWEST & THE GREAT LAKES ST LOUIS

Kansas City

POP 489,000

With its fiery barbecues (100-plus joints smoke it up), bubbling fountains (more than 200; on par with Rome) and blaring jazz, Kansas City is one of America's most appealing cities. It's certainly a don't-miss Great Plains highlight with world-class museums and quirky art-filled neighborhoods that jostle for your attention. You can easily run aground for several days as you tune into the local vibe.

◉ Sights & Activities

State Line Rd divides KCMO (Kansas City, MO) and KCK (Kansas City, KS). The latter is a bland swath of suburban sprawl with little to offer travelers. KCMO has some distinct areas, including the art-deco-filled downtown.

★ Negro Leagues Baseball Museum
MUSEUM

(☑ 816-221-1920; www.nlbm.com; 1616 E 18th St; adult/child $10/6; ☉ 9am-6pm Tue-Sat, from noon Sun) This comprehensive museum covers the lesser-known history of African American teams, such as the KC Monarchs and New York Black Yankees, that flourished until baseball became fully integrated. It's part of the Museums at 18th & Vine complex.

★ National WWI Museum
MUSEUM

(☑ 816-888-8100; www.theworldwar.org; 2 Memorial Dr; adult/child $18/10; ☉ 10am-5pm daily Jun-Aug, Tue-Sun Sep-May; ℗) Enter this impressive modern museum on a glass walkway over a field of red poppies, the symbol of remembrance of WWI. Through detailed and engaging displays, learn about a war that is almost forgotten by many Americans. The only quibble is that military hardware and uniforms take precedence over the horrible toll of the trench fighting. The museum is crowned by the historic Liberty Memorial, which has sweeping views over the city.

★ Nelson-Atkins Museum of Art
MUSEUM

(☑ 816-751-1278; www.nelson-atkins.org; 4525 Oak St; ☉ 10am-5pm Mon, Wed, Sat & Sun, to 9pm Thu & Fri; ℗) FREE Giant badminton shuttlecocks (the building represents the net) surround this encyclopedic museum, which has standout European painting, photography and Asian art collections. With free entry, a gorgeous sculpture garden and an expansive collection from top-tier artists, what's not to like? Blockbuster special exhibits carry admission fees.

Kansas City Walking Tours
WALKING

(☑ 816-725-0794; www.kcwalkingtours.com; 200 Main St; tours from $48) Walking tours of River Market, including a themed food tour that takes two hours and does a deep dive at City Market and the surrounding blocks. Other tours utilize the excellent KC Streetcar to explore the city.

★☆ Festivals & Events

American Royal World Series of Barbecue
FOOD & DRINK

(www.americanroyal.com; 400 Speedway Blvd, Kansas Speedway; tickets $6-55; ☉ Sep) For over 40 years, the world's largest barbecue contest has taken over Kansas City for one weekend, with more than 500 international teams in competition.

🛏 Sleeping

★ Jefferson House B&B
B&B $$

(☑ 816-673-6291; www.jeffersonhousekc.com; 1728 Jefferson St; r $155-195; ℗ ❄ 🛜) Jefferson House is funkier than most Missouri mansion-cum-B&Bs, with a mix of modern and classic touches. There are just three rooms and one has sweeping city views. It's the kind of home you'd live in if you had exquisite taste. Stylish touches abound; breakfasts are excellent.

Aladdin
BOUTIQUE HOTEL $$

(☑ 816-421-8888; www.hialaddin.com; 1215 Wyandotte St; r $120-220; ❄ 🛜) Affiliated with Holiday Inn, this 16-story hotel dates from 1925. It has been restored to its Italian Romanesque splendor and has 193 compact yet

---

TOURING THE FOUNTAINS

Spraying their streams large and small, Kansas City's more than 200 fountains are beautiful amenities and many are truly spectacular works of art. The website for the City of Fountains Foundation (www.kcfountains.com) is a great resource, with maps, info and downloadable self-guided tours. Among the best are JC Nichols Memorial Fountain, near Country Club Plaza, and the Crown Center Square Fountain.

stylish rooms. It was a legendary haunt of mobsters and Greta Garbo. Not your ordinary chain hotel.

Southmoreland on the Plaza B&B $$

(☑816-531-7979; www.southmoreland.com; 116 E 46th St, Country Club Plaza; r $130-250; P☀️🛜) The 12 rooms at this posh B&B are furnished like the home of your rich country-club friends. It's a big old mansion between the art museums and the Plaza (☑816-753-0100; www.countryclubplaza.com). Extras include Jacuzzis, sherry, a fireplace and more. Some rooms have outside sitting areas, others are snug.

✕ Eating

★ Betty Rae's Ice Cream ICE CREAM $

(☑816-214-8753; www.bettyraes.com; 412 Delaware St; from $4; ⏱11am-10pm Sun-Thu, to 11pm Fri & Sat; 🐾) The best ice cream in the Great Plains? Could be. Choose from 25 flavors of sensationally creamy ice cream, including the remarkable lavender honey. After surviving the queue, relax on the tree-shaded patio.

★ Golden Ox STEAK $$

(☑816-842-2866; www.goldenoxkc.com; 1600 Genessee St; mains $12-60; ⏱5-10pm Tue-Sat, 4-9pm Sun) In 1949, when this riverfront strip was the site of the KC stockyards, the Golden Ox served its first steak. Over the years it became a local legend for serving the very best cuts of beef. Even after the stockyards were demolished, the Ox soldiered on. Recently it's had a makeover and once again serves KC's best steak.

🍷 Drinking & Nightlife

Up-Down BAR

(☑816-982-9455; www.updownkc.com; 101 Southwest Blvd; ⏱3pm-1am Mon-Fri, 11am-1am Sat, 11am-midnight Sun) A popular bar-cum-playground just south of downtown, Up-Down caters to the kid in everyone with an array of games from pinball to video. There are huge decks and great music. The superb tap-beer lineup includes all the beers from Boulevard Brewery (☑816-474-7095; www.boulevard.com; 2501 Southwest Blvd; tours from $5; ⏱11am-8pm Mon-Thu, 10am-9pm Fri & Sat, to 6pm Sun), which are brewed just up the hill.

Border Brewing Co BREWERY

(☑816-315-6807; www.borderbrewco.com; 406 E 18 St; ⏱4-9pm Wed & Thu, noon-11pm Fri & Sat, noon-8pm Sun) Border brews its beers with an edge of extra hops and other flavors like citrus and berries. The line-up changes with the seasons. Its tap room in the Crossroads district is compact and welcoming. In summer the front opens up and there is a commodious deck.

Tom's Town DISTILLERY

(☑816-541-2400; www.toms-town.com; 1701 Main St; tours $10; ⏱4pm-midnight Tue-Fri, 2pm-midnight Sat, 2-10pm Sun) Tom's Town, downtown KC's first legal distillery since Prohibition, pays homage to the city's Prohibition-flouting political boss Tom Pendergast. Try the housemade vodka, gin or bourbon and let the art-deco furnishings take you back to the days when Kansas City was known as the 'Paris of the Plains.' Creative small bites are on the menu.

GREAT BARBECUE IN KANSAS CITY

Savoring hickory-smoked brisket, pork, chicken or ribs at one of the barbecue joints around town is a must for any visitor. The local style is pit-smoked and slathered with heavily seasoned vinegar-based sauces. You may well swoon for 'burnt ends,' the crispy ends of smoked pork or beef brisket. Amazing.

Q39 (☑816-255-3753; www.q39kc.com; 1000 W 39th St; mains $9-30; ⏱11am-10pm Mon-Thu, to 11pm Fri & Sat, to 9pm Sun; P) BBQ cooking goes upmarket without losing its soul.

Arthur Bryant's (☑816-231-1123; www.arthurbryantsbbq.com; 1727 Brooklyn Ave; mains $9-16; ⏱10am-9pm Mon-Sat, 11am-8pm Sun; P) The silky, fiery sauce is reason enough for a visit.

Joe's Kansas City Bar-B-Que (☑913-722-3366; www.joeskc.com; 3002 W 47th Ave; mains $8-26; ⏱11am-9pm Mon-Sat; P) The lines outside attest to the pull of Joe's juicy pulled-pork sandwiches.

LC's Bar-B-Q (☑816-923-4484; www.lcsbarbq.com; 5800 Blue Pkwy; mains $9-22; ⏱11am-9pm Mon-Sat; P) For those who like their BBQ sauce sweet and thick.

Nelson-Atkins Museum of Art (p65)

⭐ Entertainment

The free weekly *Pitch* (www.thepitchkc.com) has the best cultural calendar.

⭐ **Mutual Musicians Foundation** JAZZ
(☑816-471-5212; www.mutualmusicianslive.com; 1823 Highland Ave; ⊙midnight-5am Sat & Sun) Near 18th and Vine in the Historic Jazz District, this former union hall for African American musicians has hosted after-hours jam sessions since 1930. Famous veteran musicians gig with young hotshots. It's friendly and pretension-free. A little bar serves cheap drinks in plastic cups. No cover charge (though a $10 donation is suggested). It only opens late on Friday and Saturday nights.

Truman Sports Complex STADIUM
(I-70 exit 9) Locals are passionate about major-league baseball's Royals (who won the World Series in 2015) and the NFL's close-but-no-cigar Chiefs. Both play at gleaming side-by-side stadiums east of the city near Independence.

ℹ️ Information

Greater Kansas City Visitor Center (☑816-691-3800; www.visitkc.com; 1321 Baltimore Ave; ⊙9am-5pm Mon-Fri, 10am-3pm Sat) Other locations include the National WWI Museum (p65) and **Union Station** (www.unionstation.org; 30 W Pershing Rd; ⊙6am-midnight).

St Joseph

POP 76,400

A major departure point for pioneers, this scruffy riverside town is a tad unkempt around the edges but has a revitalized downtown district with quirky shops and dining options filling once-abandoned storefronts. There are several compelling museums. Get details at the visitor center (p69) near I-29.

Glore Psychiatric Museum MUSEUM
See p32.

CATCHIN' THE KATY

Katy Trail State Park (☑573-449-7402; www.katytrailstatepark.com; ⊙dawn-dusk; ⊕) America's longest rail-to-trail walking and biking route starts in Machens near St Louis and St Charles and ends in Clinton, 70 miles southwest of Kansas City. Its 240 miles span the state from east to west and pass through some bucolic, sylvan countryside and atmospheric small towns. Built on an abandoned line of the Missouri-Kansas-Texas Railroad (known as the Katy), the trail has very gentle slopes, wide curves and a smooth gravel surface, making it suitable for almost everyone.

★ **Shakespeare Chateau** B&B $$
(☑816-232-2667; www.shakespearechateau.com; 809 Hall St; r $135-200; ❄️📶📺) This elegant 1885 mansion houses five spacious guest rooms upstairs and a handful of common parlors from which to soak in the opulence of yesteryear. Spread throughout are 47 stained-glass windows (look for the masterpiece in the stairwell), as well as swooping chandeliers, cherry-wood carvings and a fine art collection. Prepare to be dazzled.

Ben Magoon's Famous Delicatessen PUB FOOD $
(☑816-232-3611; www.magoonsdeli.com; 632 S 8th St; mains $7-8; ⏱11am-1:30am Mon-Sat, food until 3pm Mon-Thu, until 9pm Fri & Sat) This downtown tavern dates back to the 1920s, when the real Ben Magoon started serving what became much-loved sandwiches. The current owners carry on this tradition, including Magoon's original Reuben. Drinks are creative and include fresh ingredients; the beer list is good. On many nights there's live music.

★ **Tiger's Den** BAR
(☑816-617-2108; 519 Felix St; ⏱3-11pm Mon-Wed, from 11am Thu-Sat) Part used bookstore, part cocktail bar, Tiger's Den is the stuff of Hemingway dreams. Sit on one of the plush sofas and order a drink inspired by the contents of the all-surrounding bookshelves, including Agatha Christie's *Sparkling Cyanide* or a Tequila Mockingbird.

ROUTE 66: GET YOUR KICKS IN MISSOURI

The Show-Me State will show you a long swath of the Mother Road. Meet the route in **St Louis**, where Ted Drewes (p64) has been serving frozen custard to generations of roadies from its Route 66 location on Chippewa St. There are a couple of well-signed historic routes through the city.

Follow I-44 (the interstate is built over most of Route 66 in Missouri) on a westbound journey down the Mother Road to **Route 66 State Park** (☑636-938-7198; www.mostateparks.com; N Outer Rd, I-44 exit 266; ⏱7am-30min after sunset, museum 9am-4:30pm Mar-Nov) **FREE**, with its visitor center and museum inside a 1935 roadhouse. Although the displays show vintage scenes from around St Louis, the real intrigue here concerns the town of Times Beach, which once stood on this very site. It was contaminated with dioxin and in the 1980s the government had to raze the entire area.

Head southwest on I-44 to **Stanton** (p34), then follow the signs to family-mobbed **Meramec Caverns** (☑573-468-3166; www.americascave.com; I-44 exit 230, Stanton; adult/child $23/12; ⏱8:30am-7:30pm Jul & Aug, 9am-7pm May & Jun, reduced hours Sep-Apr; ♿), as interesting for the Civil War history and hokey charm as for the stalactites; and the conspiracy-crazy **Jesse James Wax Museum** (☑573-927-5233; www.jessejameswax museum.com; I-44 exit 230, Stanton; adult/child $10/5; ⏱9am-6pm daily Jun-Aug, 9am-5pm Sat & Sun Apr-May & Sep-Oct), which posits that James faked his death and lived until 1951.

The **Route 66 Museum & Research Center** (☑417-532-2148; www.lebanon-laclede. lib.mo.us; 915 S Jefferson Ave; ⏱8am-8pm Mon-Thu, to 5pm Fri & Sat) **FREE** at the library in **Lebanon** has memorabilia past and present. Ready for a snooze? Head to the 1940s **Munger Moss Motel** (☑417-532-3111; www.mungermoss.com; 1336 E Seminole Ave (Rte 66), near I-44 exit 130; r from $60; ❄️📶📺). It's got a monster of a neon sign and Mother Road–loving owners.

Or continue on to **Springfield** where you can stay at the iconic **Best Western Route 66 Rail Haven** (☑417-866-1963; www.bestwestern.com; 203 S Glenstone Ave; r $70-120; ❄️📶📺). Then take Hwy 96 to Civil War-era **Carthage** with its historic town square and **66 Drive-In Theatre** (☑417-359-5959; www.66drivein.com; 17231 Old 66 Blvd, Carthage; adult/child $8/4; ⏱after dusk Thu-Sun Apr-Sep; ♿). In **Joplin** get on State Hwy 66, turning onto old Route 66 (the pre-1940s route), before the Kansas state line.

The Route 66 Association of Missouri (www.missouri66.org) is a great resource. And don't miss the **Conway Welcome Center** (☑417-589-0023; I-44 Mile 110, near Conway; ⏱8am-5pm), which has an over-the-top Route 66 theme and scads of info on the historic road.

ℹ Information

St Joseph Visitor Center (☎ 816-232-1839; www.stjomo.com; 502 N Woodbine Rd, near I-29 exit 47; ⏱ 9am-3pm Mon-Fri, plus Sat Jun-Aug) Get details on the town's many museums at the visitor center near I-29.

ℹ MOUNTAIN TIME IN NORTH DAKOTA

The southwest quarter of North Dakota, including Medora, uses Mountain Time, which is one hour earlier than the rest of the state's Central Time.

IOWA

The towering bluffs on the Mississippi River and the soaring Loess Hills lining the Missouri River bookend the rolling farmland of this bucolic state. In the middle you'll find the writers' town of Iowa City, the commune dwellers of the Amana Colonies, and plenty of picture-perfect rural towns, including those amid the covered bridges of Madison County.

Iowa emerges from slumber every four years as the make-or-break state for presidential hopefuls. The Iowa Caucus opens the national election battle, and wins by George W Bush in 2000 and Barack Obama in 2008 stunned many pundits and launched their victorious campaigns.

ℹ Information

Iowa Tourism Office (www.traveliowa.com)

Iowa State Parks (www.iowadnr.gov) State parks are free to visit.

Sioux City

POP 82,600

Right on the Missouri River, Sioux City makes for a fine stop when traveling to or from South Dakota. There's an excellent museum dedicated to explorers Lewis and Clark, and some classic places to eat that date back decades, to a time when the city was still a major industrial center known for its huge stockyards (now mostly closed).

Lewis & Clark Interpretive Center MUSEUM
See p32.

Tastee Inn & Out FAST FOOD $
(☎ 712-255-0857; www.tasteeinnandout.com; 2610 Gordon Dr; mains $4-7; ⏱ 11am-11pm Sun-Thu, to midnight Fri & Sat) Run by the Calligan family since 1955, this Sioux City institution is a true drive-in (the only interior seating is the seats in your car). There are two specials here. One is the Tastee, an Iowa loosemeat sandwich (a much-loved regional specialty that combines loose ground beef, onions and orange cheese). The other is onion chips, which are battered and fried.

NORTH DAKOTA

Fields of grain – green in spring and summer, bronze in fall and white in winter – stretch beyond every horizon in much of desolate North Dakota. Except for the rugged 'badlands' of the far west, geographic relief is subtle; often it's the collapsing remains of a failed homestead that break up the vista.

This is one of the least-visited states in the US. However the lack of holiday-makers doesn't mean the state is a sleepy backwater. The Bakken oil boom (named for geologic formations beneath the surface) has transformed the northwest quadrant into one vast drilling site. At night, fires burning off waste gas give the landscape hellish vistas. Once sleepy towns like Williston (p34) and Watford City have been transformed into industrial warrens.

Near the Montana border you'll find natural beauty that justifies a trip while the Missouri River is dotted with sights tied to the Lewis and Clark Expedition.

ℹ Information

North Dakota Tourism (www.ndtourism.com)

North Dakota Bed & Breakfast Association (www.ndbba.com)

North Dakota State Parks (www.parkrec. nd.gov) Vehicle entrance fees cost $7/35 per day/year.

SOUTH DAKOTA

Gently rolling prairies through shallow fertile valleys mark much of this endlessly attractive state. But head southwest and all hell breaks loose – in the best possible way. The Badlands National Park is the geologic equivalent of fireworks. The Black Hills are like opera: majestic, challenging, intriguing and even frustrating. Mt Rushmore (p20) matches the Statue of Liberty for five-star icon status.

❶ Information

South Dakota Department of Tourism (www.travelsd.com)

Bed & Breakfast Innkeepers of South Dakota (www.southdakotabb.com)

South Dakota State Parks (www.gfp.sd.gov) Vehicle permits cost $6/30 per day/year.

Pierre

POP 14,000

Pierre (pronounced 'peer') boasts a scenic location on the Missouri River and makes a decent stopover in the middle of South Dakota. It's the capital of South Dakota, but it's just too small to feel like the seat of power.

Getting here is more than half the fun: the **Native American Scenic Byway** (www.scenicbyways.info) begins in Chamberlain on Hwy 50 and meanders 100 crooked miles following the Missouri River through rolling, rugged countryside northwest to Pierre. It mostly follows Hwy 1806.

South Dakota Cultural Heritage Center MUSEUM
See p33.

Hitching Horse Inn B&B $
(🖉 605-494-0550; 635 N Euclid Ave; r $60-100; ❄️🛜) This welcoming four-room inn has an understated charm and is free of the suffocating twee doodads common in other B&Bs. Two of the rooms have Jacuzzi tubs and there's

a tiny equestrian-themed beer and wine bar on the 1st floor that's popular with locals.

Cattleman's Club STEAK $$
(🖉 605-224-9774; www.cattlemansclubsteakhouse.com; 29608 Hwy 34; mains $8-35; ⊙5-10pm Mon-Sat) Offering a gorgeous view over the Missouri River, this famed steakhouse 6 miles east of Pierre hopes you won't order your hunk of beef well done (enjoy it pink and juicy!).

Black Hills

They call the Black Hills an evergreen island in a sea of high-prairie grassland. This stunning region on the Wyoming–South Dakota border lures scores of visitors with its winding canyons and wildly eroded 7000ft peaks. The region's name – the 'Black' comes from the dark ponderosa-pine-covered slopes – was conferred by the Lakota Sioux. In the 1868 Fort Laramie Treaty, they were assured that the hills would be theirs for eternity, but the discovery of gold changed that and the Sioux were shoved out to low-value flatlands only six years later. The 1990 film *Dances with Wolves* covers some of this period.

You'll need several days to explore the bucolic back-road drives, caves, bison herds, forests, Deadwood, and Mt Rushmore and Crazy Horse monuments, and to experience the abundant outdoor ac-

Dinosaur statue, Rapid City

LOGAN BUSH/SHUTTERSTOCK ©

tivities (cycling, rock climbing, boating, hiking, downhill skiing, gold-panning etc). Like fool's gold, gaudy tourist traps lurk in corners.

ℹ️ Information

Avoid visiting during the Sturgis Motorcycle Rally (p25) in early August, when hogs rule the roads and fill the rooms. Much is closed October to April.

Black Hills Visitor Center (☑ 605-355-3700; www.blackhillsbadlands.com; I-90 exit 61, Rapid City, 1851 Discovery Circle; ⊗ 8am-7pm Jun-Aug, to 5pm Sep-May; 🛜) has tons of info. Ask about various informative and useful apps on offer.

ℹ️ Getting There & Around

Rapid City Regional Airport (RAP; ☑ 605-394-4195; www.rapairport.com; 4550 Terminal Rd) is 9 miles southeast of Rapid City. It's the main gateway for trips into the Badlands and Black Hills, and has services from major American hubs. Jefferson Lines (www.jefferson lines.com) buses travel along I-90, east to Sioux Falls ($74, six hours, one daily) and west into Wyoming.

There is no public transportation to (or within) the Black Hills so it's best to visit the region with your own wheels.

Rapid City

POP 74,500

An appealing capital to the region, 'Rapid' has a cosmopolitan air and is a good urban base for Black Hills exploration, particularly for those who enjoy their creature comforts.

👁️ Sights

Get a walking-tour brochure of Rapid's historic buildings and public art from the Black Hills Visitor Center or the city's visitor center (p72). Check out the watery fun and regular events downtown on **Main St Square**. Nearby, visit **Art Alley** (north of Main St between 6th and 7th Sts), where urban-style graffiti and pop art has turned a mundane alley into a kaleidoscope of color. And besides presidents, look for **statues of dinosaurs** around town.

Family-friendly and proudly hokey tourist attractions vie for dollars along Hwy 16 on the way to Mt Rushmore.

⭐ Statues of Presidents   STATUE

(www.presidentsrc.com; 631 Main St; ⊗ info center noon-9pm Mon-Sat May-Sep, shorter hours other times) FREE From a shifty-eyed Nixon

in repose to a triumphant Harry Truman, lifelike statues dot corners throughout the center of Rapid City. Maps are available online and at the friendly info center on Main St (which also sells ice cream). The much-anticipated statue for Barack Obama debuted at the corner of St Joseph and Fourth Sts in 2019.

Journey Museum & Learning Center   MUSEUM

(☑ 605-394-6923; www.journeymuseum.org; 222 New York St; adult/child $12/7; ⊗ 9am-6pm Mon-Sat, 11am-5pm Sun May-Sep, 10am-5pm Mon-Sat, 1-5pm Sun Oct-Apr; ♿) This impressive downtown facility is four museums in one, looking at the history of the region from prehistoric times until today. Collections come from the vaunted Museum of Geology (p19), the Sioux Indian Museum, the Minnilusa Pioneer Museum and the South Dakota Archaeological Research Center.

🛏️ Sleeping

Rushmore Hotel & Suites   HOTEL $$

(☑ 605-348-8300; www.therushmorehotel.com; 445 Mt Rushmore Rd; r $100-200; 🅿️✳️@🛜🐾) 🐾 This high-rise hotel has been transformed into a high-concept downtown gem with ecofriendly accents. A lot of the furniture is made from recycled materials, yet there's no skimping on comfort. The marble floor in the lobby is a stunner.

⭐ Hotel Alex Johnson   HISTORIC HOTEL $$$

(☑ 605-342-1210; www.alexjohnson.com; 523 6th St; r $150-300; ✳️@🛜) The design of this 1927 classic magically blends Germanic Tudor architecture with traditional Lakota Sioux symbols – note the lobby's painted ceiling and the chandelier made of war lances. The rooftop bar is a delight, while the 143 rooms are modernized retro (some have fabulous views). Ask at reception about the hotel's role in Hitchcock's *North by Northwest*.

🍴 Eating

⭐ Harriet & Oak   CAFE $

(☑ 605-791-0396; www.facebook.com/harriet andoak; 329 Main St; mains $5-12; ⊗ 7am-6pm Mon-Fri, 8am-4pm Sat & Sun; 🛜) This top-notch bakery, cafe and coffee bar has a fun boho vibe. The food is tasty and healthy, especially the banana bread and the breakfast burrito on a whole-wheat tortilla. Lunchtime sandwiches are creative, and there are good microbrews on tap.

Tally's Silver Spoon
AMERICAN $$

(☎605-342-7621; www.tallyssilverspoon.com; 530 6th St; mains $15-30; ⊙7am-9pm) Carter or Reagan? Both statues are visible out front and you can ponder your preference while you savor the upscale diner fare at this slick downtown cafe and bar. Breakfasts are always good; more creative regional fare is on offer at night. Nab a sidewalk table; on weekends there's live music. Great service.

🛍 Shopping

⭐ Prairie Edge
ARTS & CRAFTS

(☎605-342-3408; www.prairieedge.com; 606 Main St; ⊙9am-7pm Mon-Sat, 11am-5pm Sun May-Sep, shorter hours other times) This labyrinthine three-story shop has a truly mesmerizing collection of art, furniture and home goods made by members of the Northern Plains tribes. You'll also find out-of-print books and supplies to make your own Native American–inspired works. The upstairs galleries have better items on display than you'll find in many regional museums.

ℹ Information

Rapid City Visitor Information Center (www.visitrapidcity.com; 512 Main St, Main Street Square; ⊙8am-5pm Mon-Fri) A helpful resource located on Main Street Square.

Deadwood

POP 1300

Once the very definition of lawless, this town built on gold attracts a different kind of fortune seeker these days, with dozens of gambling halls big and small that would no doubt put a sly grin on the faces of the hard characters who once stomped these grounds. Then again, losers' largesse is paying for Deadwood's restoration, which makes it a fascinating place to explore, especially if you can ignore the, er, gamier aspects of mass tourism.

Settled illegally by eager gold rushers in the 1870s, Deadwood is now a National Historic Landmark.

⊙ Sights

⭐ Mt Moriah Cemetery
CEMETERY

(☎605-578-2600; 2 Mt Moriah Dr; adult/child $2/free, tours $10/5; ⊙8am-6pm Jun-Aug, dawn-dusk Sep-May) Calamity Jane (born Martha Jane Burke; 1852–1903) and Wild Bill Hickok (1837–76) rest side by side up on Boot Hill at this very steep cemetery. Pick up the map and explore. Bus tours stop here.

Adams Museum
MUSEUM

(☎605-578-1714; www.deadwoodhistory.com; 54 Sherman St; by donation adult/child $5/2; ⊙9am-5pm May-Sep, 10am-4pm Tue-Sun Oct-Apr) This revitalized museum does an excellent job of capturing the town's colorful past. There's also a small store with books on the region.

🛏 Sleeping & Eating

Bullock Hotel
HISTORIC HOTEL $$

(☎605-578-1745; www.historicbullock.com; 633 Main St; r $90-200; ❄🛜) Fans of the *Deadwood* TV show will recall the conflicted but upstanding sheriff Seth Bullock. This hotel was opened by the real Bullock in 1895. The 28 rooms are modern while retaining the building's period charm. Like most hotels here, it has a casino.

Deadwood Social Club
ITALIAN $$

(☎800-952-9398; www.saloon10.com; 657 Main St; mains $20-30; ⊙11am-9pm Sun-Thu, to 10pm Fri & Sat) Housed with the historic **Saloon No 10** (⊙kitchen 11am-9pm, bar 9am-2am), this busy restaurant offers crowd-pleasing Italian fare plus steaks. The wine list is long and you can enjoy a drink or a meal under the stars on the rooftop deck.

ℹ Information

Deadwood History & Information Center (☎800-999-1876; www.deadwood.com; 3 Siever St; ⊙8am-7pm Jun-Aug, 9am-5pm Sep-May) This splendid center in the restored train depot has tons of local tourist info, plus exhibits and photos of the town's history. Pick up the walking tour brochure.

Lead

POP 3000

Steeply uphill from Deadwood, Lead (pronounced 'leed') has an unpolished charm and still bears plenty of scars from the mining era. Yet now there's also whiffs of gentrification, as white-jumpsuit-clad physicists conducting experiments deep in the old mines have replaced rough-edged miners. It makes a solid base for skiing at nearby resorts during the winter season.

The historic walking tour brochure is freely available around town and provides guidance for a great walk.

Sanford Lab Homestake Visitor Center
MINE

(☑605-584-3110; www.sanfordlabhomestake.com; 160 W Main St; viewing area free, tours adult/child $10/8; ⊘9am-5pm) Gape at the 1250ft-deep Homestake Gold Mine to see what open-pit mining can do to a mountain. Nearby are the mine's shafts, which plunge more than 1.5 miles below the surface and are now being used for physics research, explained through exhibits in the visitor center. For $10 you can whack golf balls into the seemingly bottomless pit from the observation deck.

★Town Hall Inn
HISTORIC HOTEL $

(☑605-584-1112; www.townhallinn.com; 215 W Main St; r $60-160; ☏) This 12-room inn occupies the 1912 Town Hall and has spacious suites named and themed in honor of their former purpose, from the municipal judges chamber to the jury room and mayor's office.

Black Hills National Forest

The majority of the Black Hills lie within this 1.2-million-acre mixture of protected and logged forest, perforated by pockets of private land on most roads. The scenery is fantastic, whether you get deep into it on the 450 miles of hiking trails or drive the byways and gravel fire roads.

★George S Mickelson Trail
HIKING

(☑605-584-3896; www.mickelsontrail.com; day/annual pass $4/15) The 109-mile George S Mickelson Trail cuts through much of the Black Hills forest, running from Deadwood through Hill City and Custer to Edgemont on an abandoned railway line. There are bike rentals at various trailside towns and 15 trailheads along the way. Download a useful trail guide from the website.

🛏 Sleeping

Good camping abounds in the forest. There are 30 basic campgrounds (sites $14 to $25; no showers or electricity) and cabins ($35); reserve in summer (☑877-444-6777, www.recreation.gov). Free backcountry camping is allowed just about anywhere; no open fires.

Spearfish Canyon Lodge
LODGE $$

(☑605-584-3435; www.spfcanyon.com; 10619 Roughlock Falls Rd, off US 14A, Lead; r $90-260; ❋☏❄) This rural retreat is 13 miles south of Spearfish near trails and streams. The lodge's massive lobby fireplace adds charm

WORTH A TRIP

WIND CAVE NATIONAL PARK

Wind Cave National Park (☑605-745-4600; www.nps.gov/wica; off US 385; admission free; ⊘visitor center 8am-7pm Jun–mid-Aug, reduced hours mid-Aug–May) This park, protecting 44 sq miles of grassland and forest, sits just south of Custer State Park (p74). The central draw is, of course, the cave; the strong wind gusts, which are felt at the entrance, but not inside, give the cave its name. The visitor center has details on the variety of tours that are offered, from one-hour candlelit walks to four-hour crawls.

and the 54 modern piney rooms are cozy. There's a hot tub on a deck.

ℹ Information

Pactola Visitor Center (☑605-343-8755; www.fs.usda.gov/blackhills; US 385, near Hwy 44; ⊘9am-5pm mid-May–Aug) A modern visitor center overlooking the Pactola Reservoir between Hill City and Rapid City. It's a scenic spot for a picnic.

Hill City
POP 1000

One of the more appealing towns up in the hills, Hill City is less frenzied than places such as Keystone, though it virtually shuts down outside of the summer season. Its main drag has cafes, many galleries, cutesy candy shops and Western outfitters.

★1880 Train
TOURS

(☑605-574-2222; www.1880train.com; 222 Railroad Ave, Hill City; adult/child round-trip $32/16; ⊘mid-May–Dec) This classic steam train runs 10 miles through rugged country to Hill City from Keystone. There are one to five departures each way daily. A train museum is next door.

Alpine Inn
HISTORIC HOTEL $$

(☑605-519-9163; www.alpineinnhillcity.com; 133 Main St; r $85-150; ⊘restaurant 11am-2:30pm & 5-9pm; ☏) Right in the center of town, the Alpine Inn dates to 1884 and has comfy rooms in regal red. The restaurant serves filling German-accented fare (mains $8 to $15).

Custer State Park

Custer State Park (☎605-255-4515; https://gfp.sd.gov/parks/detail/custer-state-park; 7-day pass per car $20; ⊙24hr) boasts one of the largest free-roaming bison herds in the world (about 1500), the famous 'begging burros' (donkeys seeking handouts) and more than 200 bird species. Other wildlife include elk, pronghorns, mountain goats, bighorn sheep, coyotes, prairie dogs, mountain lions and bobcats.

The park has five impressive resorts (www.custerresorts.com) – book well ahead – and nine campgrounds (tent sites $19 to $35). At four of the campgrounds, you can rent a well-equipped camping cabin ($50). Sylvan Lake is the most scenic (and popular) campground so reserve well ahead (via www.campsd.com). Reservations are vital for all sites in summer. Backcountry camping ($7 per person per night) is allowed only in the French Creek Natural Area.

ℹ Information

Located on the east side of Custer State Park, the Custer State Park Visitor Center (p21) has good exhibits and offers activities such as guided nature walks.

Custer City

POP 1900

Custer City (or just Custer) is a major Black Hills hub, at the junction of US 16 and US 385. On the downside, its main drag is busy with traffic. On the upside, it has a good selection of places to eat and stay plus one of the region's best visitor centers. It's close to Custer State Park and Mt Rushmore (p20).

◉ Sights

Crazy Horse Memorial　　　　　MONUMENT
See p24.

Jewel Cave National Monument　　　CAVE
See p24.

🛏 Sleeping

Rocket Motel　　　　　　　　　MOTEL $
(☎605-673-4401; www.rocketmotel.com; 211 Mt Rushmore Rd; r $60-160; ❄ 🛜) The jaunty neon sign out front alone makes this old-style motor court a good option. However, it's also well located in the center, is well maintained and has great prices. As they say, 'It's a blast from the past!'

ℹ Information

Visitor Center (☎605-673-2244; www.custersd.com; 615 Washington St; ⊙8am-5pm Mon-Fri, 9am-5pm Sat, 10am-4pm Sun) The best tourist office in the Black Hills can help with any question. Reams of brochures and reading material.

NEBRASKA

The Cornhusker State (they do grow a lot of ears) has beautiful river valleys and an often stark bleakness that is entrancing. Its links to the past – from vast fields of dinosaur remains to Native American culture to the toils of hardy settlers – provide a dramatic story line. Alongside the state's sprinkling of cute little towns, Nebraska's two main cities, Omaha and Lincoln, are vibrant and artful.

The key to enjoying this long, stoic stretch of country is to take the smaller roads, whether it's US 30 instead of I-80, US 20 to the Black Hills, or the lonely and magnificent US 2.

ℹ Information

Nebraska Tourism Commission (www.visitnebraska.com)

Nebraska Association of Bed & Breakfasts (www.nebraskabb.com)

Nebraska State Parks (www.outdoornebraska.gov) Vehicle permits cost on average $8/46 per day/year.

Omaha

POP 466,900

Don't plan a quick pit stop in Omaha. Home to the brick-and-cobblestoned Old Market neighborhood, a booming riverfront, a lively food and music scene and several good museums, a few hours can turn into a few days in this town.

Omaha grew to prominence as a transport hub. Its location on the Missouri River and proximity to the Platte River made it an important stop on the Oregon, California and Mormon Trails, and later the Union Pacific Railroad stretched west from here. These days Omaha is in the nation's top 10 for billionaires and Fortune 500 companies per capita. Money pours back into the city in spectacular ways thanks to several wealthy benefactors (including famed investor Warren Buffett).

MICHAEL GORDON/SHUTTERSTOCK ©

Bison, Custer State Park

⊙ Sights

★**Riverfront**   WATERFRONT
See p32

★**Union Pacific Railroad
Museum**   MUSEUM
(✐712-329-8307; www.uprrmuseum.org; 200 Pearl St, Council Bluffs; ⊙by reservation 10am-4pm Thu-Sat; ⊛) **FREE** Just across the river from Omaha in the cute little downtown area of Council Bluffs, IA, this highly interactive museum tells the story of the world's most profitable railroad (it's headquartered in Omaha) and the company that rammed the transcontinental line west from here in the 1860s. The three levels of exhibits offer a nostalgia-filled ode to train travel and how it forever changed America.

★**Omaha's Henry Doorly
Zoo & Aquarium**   ZOO
(✐402-733-8401; www.omahazoo.com; 3701 S 10th St; adult/child $22/16 May-Sep, reduced admission other times; ⊙9am-6pm Apr-Oct, 10am-5pm Nov-Mar; ⊛) The world's largest indoor desert? Check. The world's largest nocturnal exhibit? Check. America's largest indoor rainforest? Check. An aquarium showing habitats from the Arctic to coral reefs? Check, yet again. The superlatives say it all. You could easily spend an entire day wandering through this massive and well-crafted complex, which is frequently named the best zoo in America. Optional

animal encounters can be arranged if you pay extra.

Durham Museum   MUSEUM
(✐402-444-5071; www.durhammuseum.org; 801 S 10th St; adult/child $11/7; ⊙by reservation 10am-4pm Tue-Sat, noon-4pm Sun) The soaring art-deco Union Station train depot is a sight to behold with its cathedral windows, geometric chandeliers, ornate ceilings and reliefs of railroad workers carved into the facade. It houses a fine museum covering local history from the Lewis and Clark expedition to the Omaha stockyards and the trains that once called here. The soda fountain still serves hot dogs and phosphate sodas.

↪ Tours

★**Nebraska Tour Company**   TOURS
(✐402-881-3548; www.nebraskatourcompany.com; tours from $30) Walking tours, brewery or winery-hopping trips and off-the-beaten-path excursions to Omaha's hidden treasures are among the tours offered by this excellent operator. History and art tours are led by local experts. A jaunt around Old Market is one of its most popular walking tours.

🛏 Sleeping

★**Hotel Deco**   HISTORIC HOTEL $$
(✐402-991-4981; www.hoteldecoomaha.com; 1504 Harney St; r from $140; ⊛🖘) This

soaring hotel is in a repurposed 1930 commercial building that, as the name implies, was designed in sleek art deco style. Rooms are very comfortable and decorated in a period palette of silver, grey, black and white. The public spaces are grand and the house steakhouse Monarch is well-regarded.

Magnolia Hotel HISTORIC HOTEL **$$**
(☑ 402-341-2500; www.magnoliahotelomaha.com; 1615 Howard St; r $140-250; ✲◉☎☀) Not far from Old Market, the Magnolia is a boutique hotel housed in a restored 1923 Italianate high-rise. The 145 rooms have a vibrant, modern style. Get ready for bedtime milk and cookies.

✗ Eating & Drinking

★ **Johnny's Cafe** STEAK **$$**
(☑ 402-731-4774; www.johnnyscafe.com; 4702 S 27th St; mains $15-35; ◷ 11am-2pm Tue-Fri, 5-9pm Tue-Thu, to 10pm Fri & Sat) The same family has been running this local legend of a steakhouse since 1922. The restaurant itself is a living museum of decor, with custom artwork spread throughout the lavish 1950s interior (they'll give you a tour, just ask). Settle into one of the plush chairs on casters and select from a superb line-up of steaks and other meaty mains.

AIR FORCE IN OMAHA
••
If you see large military planes drifting slowly across the sky, they're likely headed for one of the Omaha region's large air-force bases.

After WWII Omaha's Offutt Air Force Base was home to the US Air Force Strategic Air Command, the nuclear force detailed in *Dr Strangelove*. This legacy is documented at the cavernous **Strategic Air Command & Aerospace Museum** (☑ 402-944-3100; www.sacmuseum.org; 28210 West Park Hwy, I-80 exit 426; adult/child $12/6; ◷ 9am-5pm), which bulges with bombers, from the B-17 to the B-52 to the B-1. Don't expect exhibits looking at the wider implications of bombing. It's 30 miles southwest of Omaha, well within the kill radius of a 1-megaton bomb.

A perfect meal: the trademark onion rings, the house salad with blue cheese and the Omaha strip steak. Portions are vast.

Upstream Brewing Company AMERICAN **$$**
(☑ 402-344-0200; www.upstreambrewing.com; 514 S 11th St; mains $10-30; ◷ 11am-10pm Mon-Thu, 11am-11pm Fri, 8am-11pm Sat, 10am-9pm Sun) In a big old firehouse in Old Market, the beer here is equally big on flavor. The Caesar salads have enough garlic to propel you over the Missouri to Iowa. Steaks are thick and up to local standards. There are sidewalk tables, a rooftop deck and a huge bar.

Au Courant Restaurant BISTRO **$$**
(☑ 402-505-9917; www.aucourantrestaurant.com; 6064 Maple St; mains $13-27; ◷ 5pm-late Tue-Sat) Farm-fresh fare with a French accent is served in this artful restaurant. The bar is a real draw; after the last meal is served, people linger, enjoying the creative cocktails. Au Courant is a star among many in the Benson neighborhood.

★ **Mister Toad's** PUB
(☑ 402-345-4488; www.mrtoadspub.com; 1002 Howard St; ◷ 2pm-2am Sun-Fri, noon-2am Sat) Sit out front on benches under big trees or nab a corner table inside. It's woodsy, worn and flirting with dive-bar status. There's live jazz Sunday nights and Ray Williams on the piano Wednesday nights.

🛍 Shopping

Omaha Farmers Market MARKET
(www.omahafarmersmarket.com; cnr 11th & Jackson Sts; ◷ 8am-12:30pm Sat May–mid-Oct; ✈) Dozens of vendors celebrate the best of Nebraska's farms and food producers at this huge and popular market fittingly located in Old Market. Besides exquisite produce, look for baked goods and prepared foods plus crafts by artisans.

ⓘ Information

Omaha Visitor Center (☑ 866-937-6624; www.visitomaha.com; 1001 Farnam St; ◷ 9am-4:30pm Mon-Fri, 10am-4pm Sat, 10am-2pm Sun; ☎) Close to Old Market, has info for the entire region.

ILLINOIS

Chicago dominates the state with its sky-high architecture and superlative museums, restaurants and music clubs. But venturing further afield reveals Oak Park, Hemingway's mannerly hometown, scattered shrines to local hero Abe Lincoln, and a trail of corn dogs, pies and drive-in movie theaters down Route 66. A cypress swamp and a prehistoric World Heritage Site make appearances in Illinois too.

Chicago

POP 2.72 MILLION

Steely skyscrapers, top chefs, rocking festivals – the Windy City will blow you away with its low-key cultured awesomeness.

It's hard to know what to gawk at first. High-flying architecture is everywhere, from the stratospheric, glass-floored Willis Tower to Frank Gehry's swooping silver Pritzker Pavilion to Frank Lloyd Wright's stained-glass Robie House. Whimsical public art studs the streets; you might be walking along and wham, there's an abstract Picasso statue that's not only cool to look at, but you're allowed to go right up and climb on it. For art museums, take your pick: impressionist masterpieces at the massive Art Institute, psychedelic paintings at the midsized Museum of Mexican Art or outsider drawings at the small Intuit gallery.

History

Much of Chicago's past is downright legendary. You've probably heard about Mrs O'Leary's cow that kicked over a lantern that started the Great Fire that torched the city. And about a man named Al Capone who wielded a mean machine gun during an unsavory era of booze-fueled vice. And about the 'machine' that has controlled local politics for decades. Throw in the invention of the skyscraper and Ferris wheel, and you've got a whopper of a tale.

⊙ Sights

Big-ticket draws such as Millennium Park, Willis Tower and the Art Institute are downtown right in the Loop. Next door is the lakefront Museum Campus, with three popular sights including the Field Museum (p78). To the Loop's north are Navy Pier (p78) and the 360° Chicago (p79) observatory. A short distance onward Lincoln Park (p82) and Wrigley Field (p82) do their appearance. All of these places are within a 6-mile span, and all are easy to reach on public transportation. Hyde Park is the one neighborhood with top sights that is further flung and requires some planning to reach.

All of the major attractions are open daily. Smaller museums are often closed on Monday and/or Tuesday.

⊙ The Loop

★ Art Institute of Chicago   MUSEUM
(☑312-443-3600; www.artic.edu; 111 S Michigan Ave; adult/child $25/free; ⊙by reservation 10:30am-5pm Fri-Wed, to 8pm Thu; ♿; Ⓜ Brown, Orange, Green, Purple, Pink Line to Adams) The Art Institute is the second-largest art museum in the USA. Its collection of impressionist and post-impressionist paintings rivals those in France, and the number of surrealist works is tremendous. Download the free app for DIY audio tours; it offers several quick-hit jaunts, from highlights (including Georges Seurat's *A Sunday Afternoon on the Island of La Grande Jatte* and Edward Hopper's *Nighthawks*) to architecture and pop-art tours. Allow two hours to browse the must-sees; art buffs should allocate much longer.

★ Millennium Park   PARK
(☑312-742-1168; www.millenniumpark.org; 201 E Randolph St; ⊙6am-11pm; ♿; Ⓜ Brown, Orange, Green, Purple, Pink Line to Washington/Wabash) The city's showpiece is a trove of free and arty sights. It includes Pritzker Pavilion, Frank Gehry's swooping silver band shell, which hosts free weekly concerts in summer (6:30pm; bring a picnic and bottle of wine); Anish Kapoor's beloved silvery sculpture Cloud Gate, aka the 'Bean'; and Jaume Plensa's Crown Fountain, a de facto water park that projects video images of locals spitting water, gargoyle-style.

★ Willis Tower   TOWER
(☑312-875-9696; www.theskydeck.com; 233 S Wacker Dr; adult/child $24/16; ⊙9am-10pm Mar-Sep, 10am-8pm Oct-Feb, last entry 30min prior; Ⓜ Brown, Orange, Purple, Pink Line to Quincy) It's Chicago's tallest building, and the 103rd-floor Skydeck puts you high into the heavens. Take the ear-popping, 70-second elevator ride to the top and then step onto one of the glass-floored ledges jutting out into mid-air for a knee-buckling perspective straight down. On clear days the view sweeps over four states. The entrance is on Jackson Blvd. Queues can

ℹ DISCOUNT CARDS

➡ The **Go Chicago Card** (www. smartdestinations.com/chicago) allows you to visit an unlimited number of attractions for a flat fee. It's good for one, two, three or five consecutive days. The company also offers a three-, four- or five-choice **Explorer Pass** where you pick among 29 options for sights. It's valid for 30 days. Architecture cruises, the Navy Pier Ferris wheel and all major museums are among the choices.

➡ **CityPass** (www.citypass.com/ chicago) gives access to five of the city's top draws, including the Art Institute, Shedd Aquarium and Willis Tower, over nine consecutive days. It's less flexible than Go Chicago's pass, but cheaper for those wanting a more leisurely sightseeing pace.

➡ All of the above let you skip the regular queues at sights.

take up to an hour on busy days (peak times are in summer, between 11am and 4pm Friday through Sunday).

Route 66 Sign   HISTORIC SITE
(E Adams St, btwn S Michigan & Wabash Aves; Ⓜ Brown, Orange, Green, Purple, Pink Line to Adams) Attention Route 66 buffs: the Mother Road begins in downtown Chicago. Look for the 'Historic 66 Begin' sign at the northwestern corner of Adams St and Michigan Ave, across from the Art Institute. (There's another sign at the end of the block, but this one is a replica of the original.) From Chicago the route traverses 2400 miles to Los Angeles, past neon signs, mom-and-pop motels and pie-and-coffee diners...but it all starts here.

◉ Pilsen & Near South Side

★ Field Museum of Natural History   MUSEUM
(✒ 312-922-9410; www.fieldmuseum.org; 1400 S Lake Shore Dr, Near South Side; adult/child $24/17; ⊙ 9am-5pm; ♿; ☐ 146, 130) The Field Museum houses some 30 million artifacts and includes everything but the kitchen sink – beetles, mummies, gemstones, Bushman the stuffed ape – all tended by a slew of PhD-wielding scientists, as the Field remains an active research institution. The

collection's rock star is Sue, the largest *Tyrannosaurus rex* yet discovered. She even gets her own gift shop. Special exhibits, such as the 3-D movie, cost extra.

★ National Museum of Mexican Art   MUSEUM
(✒ 312-738-1503; www.nationalmuseumofmexican art.org; 1852 W 19th St, Pilsen; ⊙ 10am-5pm Tue-Sun; Ⓜ Pink Line to 18th St) 🆓 Founded in 1982, this vibrant museum – the largest Latinx arts institution in the US – has become one of the city's best. The vivid permanent collection sums up 1000 years of Mexican art and culture through classical paintings, shining gold altars, skeleton-rich folk art, beadwork and much more.

Adler Planetarium   MUSEUM
(✒ 312-922-7827; www.adlerplanetarium.org; 1300 S Lake Shore Dr, Near South Side; adult/child $12/8; ⊙ 9:30am-4pm; ♿; ☐ 146, 130) Space enthusiasts will get a big bang (pun!) out of the Adler. There are public telescopes to view the stars (10am to 1pm daily, by the Galileo Cafe), 3-D lectures to learn about supernovas (in the **Space Visualization Lab**), and the **Planet Explorers** exhibit where kids can 'launch' a rocket. The immersive digital films cost extra (from $13 per ticket). The Adler's front steps offer Chicago's best skyline view, so get your camera ready.

Shedd Aquarium   AQUARIUM
(✒ 312-939-2438; www.sheddaquarium.org; 1200 S Lake Shore Dr, Near South Side; adult/child $40/30; ⊙ 9am-6pm Jun-Aug, 9am-5pm Mon-Fri, to 6pm Sat & Sun Sep-May; ♿; ☐ 146, 130) Top draws at the kiddie-mobbed Shedd Aquarium include the **Wild Reef** exhibit, where there's just 5in of Plexiglas between you and two-dozen fierce-looking sharks, and the **Oceanarium**, with its rescued sea otters. Note the Oceanarium also keeps beluga whales and Pacific white-sided dolphins, a practice that's increasingly frowned upon as captivity is stressful for these sensitive creatures.

◉ Near North & Navy Pier

★ Navy Pier   WATERFRONT
(✒ 312-595-7437; www.navypier.com; 600 E Grand Ave; ⊙ 10am-10pm Sun-Thu, to midnight Fri & Sat Jun-Aug, 10am-8pm Sun-Thu, to 10pm Fri & Sat Sep-May; ♿; ☐ 65) 🆓 Half-mile-long Navy Pier is one of Chicago's most-visited attractions, sporting a 196ft **Ferris wheel**

(adult/child $18/15; 🖥 65) and other carnival rides ($9 to $18 each), a beer garden and lots of chain restaurants. A renovation added public plazas, performance spaces and free cultural programming. Locals still groan over its commercialization, but its lakefront view and cool breezes can't be beat.

The fireworks displays on summer Wednesdays (9:30pm) and Saturdays (10:15pm) are a treat too.

★**Driehaus Museum**   MUSEUM
(✐312-482-8933; www.driehausmuseum.org; 40 E Erie St, River North; adult/child $20/free; ⊙10am-5pm Tue-Sun; Ⓜ Red Line to Chicago) Set in the exquisite Nickerson Mansion, the Driehaus immerses visitors in Gilded Age decorative arts and architecture. You'll feel like a *Great Gatsby* character as you wander three floors stuffed with sumptuous objets d'art and heaps of Tiffany stained glass. Recommended guided tours ($5 extra) are available four times daily. The price seems steep, but the museum is a prize for those intrigued by opulent interiors.

Magnificent Mile   AREA
(www.themagnificentmile.com; N Michigan Ave, Streeterville; Ⓜ Red Line to Grand) Spanning N Michigan Ave between the river and Oak St, the 'Mag Mile' is Chicago's much-touted upscale shopping strip, where Bloomingdale's, Apple, Burberry and many more will lighten your wallet. The retailers are mostly high-end chains that have stores nationwide.

◉ Gold Coast

★**360° Chicago**   OBSERVATORY
(✐888-875-8439; www.360chicago.com; 875 N Michigan Ave, 94th fl; adult/child $22/15; ⊙9am-11pm, last tickets 10:30pm; Ⓜ Red Line to Chicago) The views from the 94th-floor observatory of this iconic building (formerly known as the John Hancock Center) in many ways surpass those at the Willis Tower (p77); there are informative displays and the 'Tilt' feature (floor-to-ceiling windows you stand in as they tip out over the ground), which costs $7.20 extra and is less exciting than it sounds. Or just shoot straight up to the 96th-floor **Signature Lounge** (www.signatureroom.com; 875 N Michigan Ave, 96th fl; ⊙11am-12:30am Sun-Thu, to 1:30am Fri & Sat; Ⓜ Red Line to Chicago), where the view is free if you buy a drink ($10 to $18).

★**Museum of Contemporary Art**   MUSEUM
(MCA; ✐312-280-2660; www.mcachicago.org; 220 E Chicago Ave; adult/child $15/free; ⊙10am-9pm Tue & Fri, to 5pm Wed, Thu, Sat & Sun; Ⓜ Red Line to Chicago) Consider it the Art Institute's brash, rebellious sibling, with especially

Route 66 sign

Downtown Chicago

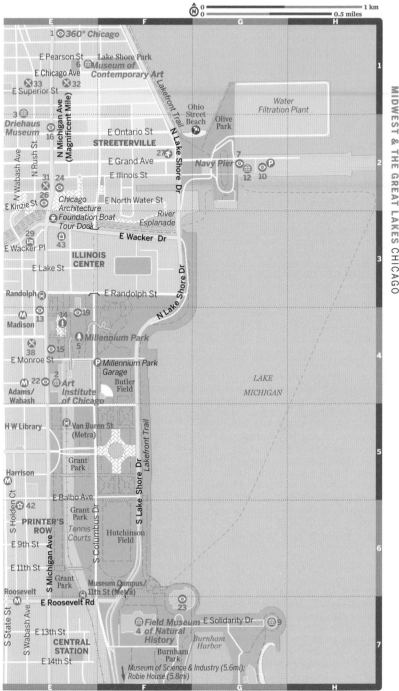

Downtown Chicago

strong minimalist, surrealist and conceptual photography collections, and permanent works by René Magritte, Cindy Sherman and Andy Warhol. Covering art from the 1920s onward, the MCA's collection spans the gamut, with displays arranged to blur the boundaries between painting, sculpture, video and other media. Exhibits change regularly so you never know what you'll see, but count on it being offbeat and provocative. Illinois residents get free admission on Tuesday.

◉ Lincoln Park & Wrigleyville

★ **Lincoln Park**   PARK
(www.chicagoparkdistrict.com; Lincoln Park; ☉6am-11pm; 🚻; 🚌22, 151, 156) The park that gave the neighborhood its name is Chicago's largest. Its 1200 acres stretch for 6 miles from North Ave north to Diversey Pkwy, where it narrows along the lake and continues on until the end of Lake Shore Dr. On sunny days locals come out to play in droves, taking advantage of the ponds,

paths and playing fields or visiting the zoo and beaches. It's a fine spot to while away a morning or afternoon (or both).

★ **Wrigley Field**   STADIUM
(☎800-843-2827; www.cubs.com; 1060 W Addison St, Wrigleyville; Ⓜ Red Line to Addison) Built in 1914 and named for the chewing-gum guy, Wrigley Field is the second-oldest baseball park in the major leagues. It's known for its hand-turned scoreboard, ivy-covered outfield walls and neon sign over the front entrance. The Cubs are the home team. Games are always packed. Ticket prices vary, but in general you'll be hard-pressed to get in for under $45. The area around the stadium is like a big street festival on game days.

◉ Logan Square & Humboldt Park

★ **Galerie F**   GALLERY
(☎872-817-7067; www.galeriefchicago.com; 2415 N Milwaukee Ave, Logan Square; ☉11am-6pm Mon &

CHICAGO IN TWO DAYS...

Day One

You might as well dive right in with the big stuff. Take a boat or walking tour with the Chicago Architecture Foundation (p84) and ogle the most sky-scraping collection of buildings the US has to offer. Saunter over to Millennium Park (p77) to see the 'Bean' reflect the skyline and to splash under Crown Fountain's human gargoyles.

Explore the Art Institute of Chicago (p77), the nation's second-largest art museum. It holds masterpieces aplenty, especially impressionist and post-impressionist paintings (and paperweights). Next, head over to Willis Tower (p77), zip up to the 103rd floor and step out onto the glass-floored ledge. Yes, it is a long way down.

The West Loop parties in the evening. Haymarket Pub & Brewery (p90) pours great beers. Or down a cocktail made with the house vodka at CH Distillery (p90).

Day Two

Take a stroll on Michigan Ave – aka the Magnificent Mile (p79) – where big-name department stores ka-ching in a glittering row. Mosey over to Navy Pier (p78). Wander the half-mile promenade and take a spin on the high-in-the-sky Ferris wheel.

Spend the afternoon at the Museum Campus (p78; the water taxi from Navy Pier is a fine way to get there). Miles of aisles of dinosaurs and gemstones stuff the Field Museum of Natural History (p78). Sharks and other fish swim in the kiddie-mobbed Shedd Aquarium (p78). Meteorites and supernovas are on view at the Adler Planetarium (p78).

Wander along Milwaukee Ave and take your pick of booming bars, indie-rock clubs and hipster shops. Quimby's (p92) shows the local spirit: the bookstore stocks zines and graphic novels, and is a linchpin of Chicago's underground culture. The Hideout (p91) and Empty Bottle (p92) are sweet spots to catch a bad-ass band.

Thu-Sun; Ⓜ Blue Line to California) Galerie F is exactly the type of laid-back, ubercool gallery you'd expect to find in Logan Square. It specializes in rock-and-roll gig posters, printmaking and street art. Walk into the bright, open space and browse – the vibe here is totally welcoming. Dip into the basement to listen to records, play chess or just linger in the sitting area.

Busy Beaver Button Museum MUSEUM
(📞773-645-3359; www.buttonmuseum.org; 3407 W Armitage Ave, Logan Square; ⊙10am-4pm Mon-Fri; 🚌73) **FREE** Even George Washington gave out campaign buttons, though in his era they were the sew-on kind. Pin-back buttons came along in 1896. Badge-making company Busy Beaver chronicles its history in displays holding thousands of the little round mementos. They tout everything from Dale Bozzio to Bozo the clown, Cabbage Patch Kids to Big Rock Point Nuclear Plant.

⊙ Hyde Park & South Side

★**Museum of Science & Industry** MUSEUM
(MSI; 📞773-684-1414; www.msichicago.org; 5700 S Lake Shore Dr, Hyde Park; adult/child $22/13; ⊙9:30am-5:30pm Jun-Aug, shorter hours Sep-May;

🚻; 🚌6 or 10, Ⓜ Metra Electric Line to 55th-56th-57th St) Geek out at the largest science museum in the Western Hemisphere. Highlights include a **WWII German U-boat** nestled in an underground display (adult/child $18/14 extra to tour it) and the **Science Storms** exhibit with a mock tornado and tsunami. Other popular exhibits include the baby chick hatchery, the minuscule furnishings in Colleen Moore's fairy castle and the life-size shaft of a coal mine (adult/child $12/9 extra to descend and tour its workings).

Robie House ARCHITECTURE
(📞312-994-4000; www.flwright.org; 5757 S Woodlawn Ave, Hyde Park; adult/child $18/15; ⊙10:30am-3pm Thu-Mon; 🚌6, Ⓜ Metra Electric Line to 59th St) Of the numerous buildings that Frank Lloyd Wright designed around Chicago, none is more famous or influential than Robie House. Because its horizontal lines resembled the flat landscape of the Midwestern prairie, the style became known as the Prairie style. Inside are 174 stained-glass windows and doors, which you'll see on the hour-long tours (frequency varies by season, but there's usually at least one tour per hour). Advance tickets are highly recommended.

CHICAGO FOR GANGSTERS

Chicago would rather not discuss its gangster past; consequently there are no brochures or exhibits about infamous sites, so you'll need to use your imagination when visiting the following places:

Green Mill (p91) Al Capone's favorite speakeasy; the tunnels where he hid the booze are still underneath the bar.

Biograph Theater (2433 N Lincoln Ave, Lincoln Park; Ⓜ Brown, Purple, Red Line to Fullerton) Where the 'lady in red' betrayed 'public enemy number one' John Dillinger.

Union Station (🗹 312-655-2385; www.chicagounionstation.com; 225 S Canal St; Ⓜ Blue Line to Clinton) Fans of *The Untouchables* can see where the baby carriage bounced down the stairs.

🏃 Activities & Tours

Chicago offers plenty of places to get active via its city-spanning shoreline, 26 beaches and 580 parks. After a long, cold winter, everyone dashes outside to play. Top marks go to the 18-mile Lakefront Trail, prime for cycling and running. Meanwhile, Lake Michigan and the Chicago River provide loads of paddling possibilities.

The flat, 18-mile **Lakefront Trail** is a beautiful ride along the water, though on nice days it's jam-packed. It starts at Ardmore Ave and rolls all the way south to 71st St. The path is split so cyclists and runners have separate lanes; look for signposts and markers painted on the ground to tell you what's what. The trail is most congested between Lincoln Park and the Museum Campus; it's least congested heading south from the museums. The Active Transportation Alliance (www.activetrans.org) publishes a bike trail map. Check @ activetransLFT on Twitter for updates on trail conditions; some parts close in bad weather.

Visitors often don't realize Chicago is a beach town, thanks to mammoth Lake Michigan lapping its side. There are 26 official strands of sand patrolled by lifeguards in summer. Swimming is popular, though the water is pretty freaking cold. Beaches at Montrose and North Ave have rental places offering kayaks and stand-up paddleboards. Other kayak companies have set up shop along the Chicago River.

★ **Bobby's Bike Hike**   CYCLING
(🗹 312-245-9300; www.bobbysbikehike.com; 540 N Lake Shore Dr, Streeterville; per hr/day from $8/27, tours $38-70; ⊙8:30am-8pm Mon-Fri, 8am-8pm Sat & Sun Jun-Aug, 9am-7pm Mar-May & Sep-Nov; Ⓜ Red Line to Grand) Locally based

Bobby's earns rave reviews from riders. It rents bikes and has easy access to the Lakefront Trail. It also offers cool tours of gangster sites, the lakefront, nighttime vistas, and venues to indulge in pizza and beer. The Tike Hike caters to kids. Enter through the covered driveway to reach the shop. Call for winter hours.

★ **Montrose Beach**   BEACH
(www.cpdbeaches.com; 4400 N Lake Shore Dr, Uptown; 🚉146) One of the city's best beaches. You can rent kayaks, stand-up paddleboards and jet skis; sometimes you'll see surfers and kitesurfers, and anglers frequently cast here. Watch sailboats glide in the harbor over some waterside snacks or a drink at the **Dock Bar and Grill**. A wide, dog-friendly beach with a curving breakwater abuts the main beach to the north.

Chicago Architecture Center Tours   TOURS
(CAC; 🗹 312-922-3432; www.architecture.org; 111 E Wacker Dr; tours $20-55) Gold-standard boat tours ($47) sail from the **river dock** (Ⓜ Brown, Orange, Green, Purple, Pink Line to State/Lake) on the southeast side of the Michigan Ave Bridge. Also popular are the Historic Skyscrapers walking tours ($26) and tours exploring individual landmark buildings ($20). CAC sponsors bus, bike and L train tours, too. Buy tickets online or at the CAC's front desk; boat tickets can also be purchased at the dock.

🎆 Festivals & Events

St Patrick's Day Parade   CULTURAL
(www.chicagostpatricksdayparade.org; ⊙mid-Mar) The local plumbers union dyes the Chicago River shamrock-green; a big parade follows downtown in Grant Park. Held the Saturday before March 17.

Chicago Blues Festival MUSIC
(www.chicagobluesfestival.us; ☉ Jun) The biggest free blues fest in the world, with three days of the music that made Chicago famous. Held in Millennium Park.

Pitchfork Music Festival MUSIC
(http://pitchforkmusicfestival.com; Union Park, Near West Side; day pass $75; ☉ mid-Jul; Ⓜ Green, Pink Line to Ashland) Taste-making alternative and emerging bands strum for three days in Union Park in mid-July.

Lollapalooza MUSIC
(www.lollapalooza.com; ☉ Aug) Up to 170 bands spill off eight stages at Grant Park's four-day mega-gig.

Chicago Marathon SPORTS
(www.chicagomarathon.com; ☉ Oct) More than 45,000 runners compete on the 26-mile course through the city's heart, cheered on by a million spectators. Held on a Sunday in October (when the weather can be pleasant or freezing), it's considered one of the world's top five marathons.

🛏 Sleeping

Chicago's lodgings rise high in the sky, many in architectural landmarks. Snooze in the building that gave birth to the skyscraper, in one of Mies van der Rohe's boxy structures, or in a century-old art deco masterpiece. Huge business hotels, trendy boutique hotels and snazzy hostels blanket the cityscape too. But nothing comes cheap...

★ **Found Hotel Chicago** HOSTEL, HOTEL $
(☎ 224-243-6863; www.foundhotels.com; 613 N Wells St, River North; dm $25-55, r $120-330; P ❄ ☎; Ⓜ Brown, Purple Line to Merchandise Mart) Breezy Found Hotel joins the elevated hostel/casual-hotel brigade. The 60 rooms come in several configurations, including four-bed dorms with sturdy (and quite comfy) bunk beds, and private rooms with twin or queen beds – all with en-suite bathrooms. Rooms are small and plain, but who cares? The price is often right, and the common areas are where the fun is.

★ **Hampton Inn Chicago Downtown/N Loop** HOTEL $$
(☎ 312-419-9014; www.hamptonchicago.com; 68 E Wacker Pl; r $200-290; P ❄ ☎; Ⓜ Brown, Orange, Green, Purple, Pink Line to State/Lake) This unique property with a central location makes you feel like a road-tripper of yore. Set in the 1928 art deco Chicago Motor Club

Building, the lobby sports a vintage Ford and a cool USA mural map from the era. The dark-wood-paneled rooms strike the right balance of retro vibe and modern amenities. Free wi-fi.

Majestic Hotel BOUTIQUE HOTEL $$
(☎ 773-404-3499; www.majestic-chicago.com; 528 W Brompton Ave, Lake View; r $159-275; P ❄ ☎; ☐ 151) Nestled into a row of residential housing, the Majestic is walking distance to Wrigley Field and Boystown and mere steps from the lakefront. From the lobby fireplace and dark-wood furnishings to the handsome, paisley-swirled decor, the interior has the cozy feel of an English manor. Free wi-fi and continental breakfast are included.

Publishing House Bed & Breakfast B&B $$
(☎ 312-554-5857; https://publishinghousebnb.com; 108 N May St, West Loop; r $179-379; Ⓜ Green, Pink Line to Morgan) The building was indeed a publishing house more than a century ago, and it's now transformed so it looks like the stylish home of your coolest city friend. The 11 warm-toned rooms, each named for a Chicago writer, have hardwood floors, mid-century modern decor and original art on the walls. A fireplace and reading nooks fill the cozy common areas.

Chicago Marathon
DOMINIQUE ROBINSON/SHUTTERSTOCK ©

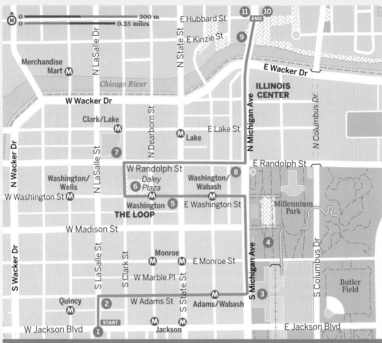

🏃 City Walk
The Loop

START CHICAGO BOARD OF TRADE
FINISH BILLY GOAT TAVERN
LENGTH 3 MILES; ABOUT TWO HOURS

This tour winds through the Loop and across the Chicago River, passing some of the city's finest old buildings and notable public art.

Start at the **1 Chicago Board of Trade** (141 W Jackson Blvd), a 1930 art-deco temple of commerce. The nearby **2 Rookery** (www. flwright.org; 209 S LaSalle St) was built in 1888 by Daniel Burnham – a monumental brick building maximizing light and air with a central atrium. Frank Lloyd Wright redesigned the lobby 19 years later.

Head east on Adams to the **3 Art Institute** (p77), one of the world's finest art museums. Just north is **4 Millennium Park** (p77), filled with avant-garde works from world-famous names such as Frank Gehry and Anish Kapoor.

Two blocks west on Washington is the 1895 **5 Reliance Building** (1 W Washington St). Another Burnham design, it's a posh ho-

tel today (it originally housed medical offices – Al Capone's dentist practiced in room 809).

Another block west is Pablo Picasso's **6 untitled sculpture** (50 W Washington St). He never revealed what it portrayed – popular guesses include a woman, a dog or a baboon – so interpret it however you like. Just northwest is another inscrutable sculpture, Jean Dubuffet's **7 Monument with Standing Beast** (100 W Randolph S).

Walk east on Randolph to beaux-arts beauty the **8 Chicago Cultural Center** (📞312-744-6630; www.chicagoculturalcenter. org; 78 E Washington St; ⏱10am-7pm Mon-Fri, to 5pm Sat & Sun) **FREE**. Further famous edifices are north of the Chicago River: the gleaming-white terra-cotta **9 Wrigley Building** (400 N Michigan Ave, Streeterville) and the neo-Gothic **10 Tribune Tower** (435 N Michigan Ave, Streeterville).

Finish up at the **11 Billy Goat Tavern**, a classic Chicago dive bar whose owner invoked the Cubs' famous curse in 1945 after being ejected from Wrigley Field because of his pet goat.

CHICAGO FOR CHILDREN

Ferocious dinosaurs at the Field Museum, an ark's worth of beasts at Lincoln Park Zoo, lakefront boat rides and sandy beaches are among the top choices for toddlin' times. Add in magical playgrounds, family cycling tours and lots of pizza, and it's clear Chicago is a kid's kind of town.

Chicago Children's Museum (☑312-527-1000; www.chicagochildrensmuseum.org; 700 E Grand Ave, Navy Pier; $15; ⊘10am-5pm, to 8pm Thu; ✦; ☐65) It is the reigning favorite, geared to kids aged 10 and under, with a slew of hands-on building, climbing and inventing exhibits. Bonus: it's located on Navy Pier.

Field Museum of Natural History (p78) Bring on the dinosaurs! The Crown Family Play-Lab, on the ground floor, lets kids excavate bones and make loads of other discoveries. It's open Thursday to Monday from 10am to 3:30pm.

Museum of Science & Industry (p83) Families could spend a week here and not see it all. Staff conduct 'experiments' in various galleries throughout the day, such as dropping things off the balcony and creating mini explosions. The Idea Factory lets scientists aged 10 and under 'research' properties of light, balance and water pressure.

Peggy Notebaert Nature Museum (☑773-755-5100; www.naturemuseum.org; 2430 N Cannon Dr, Lincoln Park; adult/child $9/6; ⊘9am-5pm Mon-Fri, from 10am Sat & Sun; ✦; ☐76, 151) This museum is somewhat overlooked, but its butterfly haven and marsh full of frogs provide gentle thrills. Bonus: it's located in Lincoln Park by the zoo.

Art Institute of Chicago (p77) The Ryan Learning Center provides interactive games (such as puzzles of famous works) and art-making activities.

★ Viceroy Chicago
LUXURY HOTEL $$$

(☑312-586-2000; www.viceroyhotelsandresorts.com; 1118 N State St; d $275-450, ste from $550; ⓟ ⊛ ✻ ⓢ ✈; ⓜRed Line to Clark/Division) The Gold Coast's newest luxury hotel, the Viceroy has 198 rooms and suites with art deco–inspired design elements with warm woods, gold accents and luxe furnishings. Blue-velvet curtains float across floor-to-ceiling windows with lake and skyline views; the restaurant, helmed by a Michelin-starred chef, features nautical yacht-club motifs. In summer you can use the rooftop dipping pool. Free wi-fi.

★ Waldorf Astoria Chicago
LUXURY HOTEL $$$

(☑312-646-1300; www.waldorfastoriachicago hotel.com; 11 E Walton St; r from $400; ⓟ ✻ @ ⓢ ✈ ✻; ⓜRed Line to Chicago) The Waldorf routinely tops the list for Chicago's best uber-luxury hotel. It models itself on 1920s Parisian glamour and, we have to admit, it delivers it in spades. Rooms are large – they have to be, to hold the fireplaces, the bars, the marble soaking tubs, the beds with 460-thread-count sheets and the fully wired work spaces and other techno gadgets.

✕ Eating

Chicago has become a chowhound's hot spot. For the most part, restaurants here are reasonably priced and pretension-free, serving masterful food in come-as-you-are environs. You can also fork into a superb range of international eats, especially if you break out of downtown and head for neighborhoods such as Pilsen or Uptown.

★ Billy Goat Tavern
BURGERS $

(☑312-222-1525; www.billygoattavern.com; 430 N Michigan Ave, lower level, Streeterville; burgers $4-8; ⊘6am-1am Mon-Thu, to 2am Fri, to 3am Sat, 9am-2am Sun; ⓜRed Line to Grand) *Tribune* and *Sun Times* reporters have guzzled in the subterranean Billy Goat for decades. Order a 'cheezborger' and Schlitz beer, then look around at the newspapered walls to get the scoop on infamous local stories, such as the Cubs' Curse. This is a tourist magnet, but a deserving one. Follow the tavern signs leading below Michigan Ave to get here.

★ Ground Control
VEGETARIAN $

(☑773-772-9446; www.groundcontrolchicago.com; 3315 W Armitage Ave, Logan Square; mains $10-12; ⊘5-10pm Tue-Thu, 5-11pm Fri, 11am-11pm Sat, 11am-9pm Sun; ✎; ☐73) Ground Control is an industrial, trippy mural-clad restaurant with pinball machines and craft beer on tap.

That it's meat-free is incidental. The dishes play off Asian, Latin and Southern flavors, like the Nashville hot tofu, sweet-potato tacos and wasabi portobello sandwich. It's super delicious, and there's always a cool-cat crowd.

Lou Mitchell's   BREAKFAST $

(☑ 312-939-3111; www.loumitchells.com; 565 W Jackson Blvd, West Loop; mains $9-14; ☺ 5:30am-3pm Mon, to 4pm Tue-Fri, 7am-4pm Sat, to 3pm Sun; ♿; Ⓜ Blue Line to Clinton) A relic of Route 66, Lou's brings in elbow-to-elbow locals and tourists for breakfast. The old-school waitstaff deliver big fluffy omelets and thick-cut French toast with a jug of syrup. They call you 'honey' and fill your coffee cup endlessly. There's often a queue to get in, but free doughnut holes and Milk Duds help ease the wait.

★ GT Fish & Oyster   SEAFOOD $$

(☑ 312-929-3501; www.gtoyster.com; 531 N Wells St, River North; mains $17-30; ☺ 5-10pm Mon-Thu, to 11pm Fri, 10am-2:30pm & 5-11pm Sat, 10am-2:30pm & 5-10pm Sun; Ⓜ Red Line to Grand) Seafood restaurants can be fusty. Not so GT Fish & Oyster. The clean-lined room bustles with date-night couples and groups of friends drinking fizzy wines and slurping mollusks. Many of the dishes are shareable, which adds to the convivial, plate-clattering ambience. The sublime clam chowder arrives in a glass jar with housemade oyster crackers and bacon.

★ Alinea   GASTRONOMY $$$

(☑ 312-867-0110; www.alinearestaurant.com; 1723 N Halsted St, Lincoln Park; 10-/16-course menus from $205/290; ☺ 5-10pm; Ⓜ Red Line to North/Clybourn) One of the world's best restaurants, the triple-Michelin-starred Alinea purveys multiple courses of molecular gastronomy. Dishes may emanate from a centrifuge or be pressed into a capsule, à la duck served with a 'pillow of lavender air.' There are no reservations; instead Alinea sells tickets two to three months in advance via its website. Check Twitter (@Alinea) for last-minute seats.

Girl & the Goat   AMERICAN $$$

(☑ 312-492-6262; www.girlandthegoat.com; 809 W Randolph St, West Loop; small plates $12-19; ☺ 4:30-11pm Sun-Thu, to midnight Fri & Sat; ☑; Ⓜ Green, Pink Line to Morgan) 🍃 Stephanie Izard's flagship restaurant rocks. The soaring ceilings, polished wood tables and cartoon-y art on the walls offer a convivial atmosphere where local beer and housemade wine hit the tables, along with unique small plates such as catfish with pickled persimmons. Reservations are difficult; try for walk-in seats before 5pm or see if anything opens up at the bar.

🍷 Drinking & Nightlife

Chicagoans love to hang out in drinking establishments. Blame it on the long winter, when folks need to huddle together some-

Billy Goat Tavern (p87), Chicago

DEEP-DISH CHICAGO

Deep-dish pizza is Chicago's most famous concoction. These behemoths are nothing like the flat circular disks known as pizza in the rest of the world. Chicago's thick-crusted pie stacks up like this: a fat and crumbly crust baked in a cast-iron pan (kind of like a skillet without a handle), capped by mozzarella, then toppings and sauce. **Gino's East** (☑ 312-266-3337; www.ginoseast.com; 162 E Superior St, Streeterville; small pizzas from $18; ⊙ 11am-9pm Sun-Thu, to 10pm Fri & Sat; M Red Line to Chicago), **Pizano's** (☑ 312-236-1777; www.pizanoschicago.com; 61 E Madison St; small pizzas from $16; ⊙ 11am-2am Sun-Fri, to 3am Sat; ☎; M Red, Blue Line to Monroe) and **Lou Malnati's** (☑ 312-828-9800; www.loumalnatis.com; 439 N Wells St, River North; small pizzas from $13; ⊙ 11am-11pm Sun-Thu, to midnight Fri & Sat; M Brown, Purple Line to Merchandise Mart) offer classic deep-dish.

An adjunct to the genre is stuffed pizza. It's like deep dish on steroids, bigger and more decadent. Basically it's dough, with cheese on top, then another layer of dough atop that, plus toppings. **Giordano's** (☑ 312-951-0747; www.giordanos.com; 730 N Rush St, River North; small pizzas from $18; ⊙ 11am-11pm Sun-Thu, to midnight Fri & Sat; M Red Line to Chicago) bakes a mighty one.

Pan pizza is the third contender. It's similar to deep dish, but the crust is baked differently so it's breadier, and it has a ring of caramelized cheese that crisps in the pan. **Pequod's** (☑ 773-327-1512; www.pequodspizza.com; 2207 N Clybourn Ave, Lincoln Park; small pizzas from $12; ⊙ 11am-2am Mon-Sat, to midnight Sun; ⬜ 9 to Webster) sets the standard for pan deliciousness.

where warm. Blame it on summer, when sunny days make beer gardens and sidewalk patios so splendid. Whatever the reason, drinking in the city is a widely cherished civic pastime.

★ **Berghoff**   BAR
(☑ 312-427-3170; www.theberghoff.com; 17 W Adams St; ⊙ 11am-9pm Mon-Fri, from 11:30am Sat; M Blue, Red Line to Jackson) The Berghoff dates from 1898 and was the first Chicago bar to serve a legal drink after Prohibition (ask to see the liquor license stamped '#1'). Little has changed around the antique wood bar since. Belly up for mugs of local and imported beers and order sauerbraten, schnitzel and pretzels the size of your head from the adjoining German restaurant.

★ **Alulu Brewery & Pub**   MICROBREWERY
(☑ 312-600-9865; www.alulubrew.com; 2011 S Laflin St, Pilsen; ⊙ 5pm-2am Mon, Wed & Thu, 3pm-2am Fri & Sun, 3pm-3am Sat; M Pink Line to 18th St) Pilsen's bohemians love this intimate brewpub and no wonder. Join them at the reclaimed wood tables for a flight and fancy pub grub such as poutine with *merguez*-sausage gravy. The brewers play around with styles, so anything from a watermelon sour to coffee blond, wheat beer or

Mexican lager may be pouring from the 20 taps when you visit.

Delilah's   BAR
(☑ 773-472-2771; www.delilahschicago.com; 2771 N Lincoln Ave, Lincoln Park; ⊙ 4pm-2am Sun-Fri, to 3am Sat; M Brown Line to Diversey) A bartender rightfully referred to this hard-edged black sheep of the neighborhood as the 'pride of Lincoln Ave': a title earned for the heavy pours and the best whiskey selection in the city – more than 860 different labels! The no-nonsense staff know their way around a beer list, too, tapping unusual domestic and international suds. Cheap Pabst longnecks are always available.

Brewing   MICROBREWERY
(☑ 773-293-6600; www.spitefulbrewing.com; 2024 W Balmoral Ave, Ravenswood; ⊙ 4-10pm Mon-Wed, to 11pm Thu, noon-midnight Fri & Sat, 11am-10pm Sun; ☎ ⬛; ⬜ 50) Spiteful's taproom has a rock-and-roll, DIY vibe. Two home brewers launched the brand, and they now operate out of a renovated garage. The concrete floored, exposed-ductwork place has a long bar where you can belly up for hard-hitting pale ales, IPAs and double IPAs.

Violet Hour   COCKTAIL BAR
(☑ 773-252-1500; www.theviolethour.com; 1520 N Damen Ave, Wicker Park; ⊙ 6pm-2am Sun-Fri,

to 3am Sat; Ⓜ Blue Line to Damen) This nouveau speakeasy isn't marked, so look for the wood-paneled building with a full mural and a yellow light over the door. Inside, high-backed booths, chandeliers and long velvet drapes provide the backdrop to elaborately engineered, award-winning seasonal cocktails with droll names. As highbrow as it sounds, friendly staff make Violet Hour welcoming and accessible.

CH Distillery   DISTILLERY
(📞312-707-8780; www.chdistillery.com; 564 W Randolph St, West Loop; ⊙4-10pm Mon-Thu, to midnight Fri & Sat; Ⓜ Green, Pink Line to Clinton) This slick tasting room has a cool, naturalistic look with exposed concrete posts and knotty wood beawms across the ceiling. Slip into a seat at the bar and watch the silver tanks behind the big glass window distilling the organic vodka and gin that go into your creative cocktail.

Haymarket Pub & Brewery   BREWERY
(📞312-638-0700; www.haymarketbeer.com; 737 W Randolph St, West Loop; ⊙11am-2am Sun-Fri, to 3am Sat; Ⓜ Green, Pink Line to Clinton) An early arrival on the West Loop scene, Haymarket remains nicely low-key. It doesn't try to win you over with uberhipness like many of its neighbors. Locals hang out in the cavernous, barrel-strewn space drinking fresh-from-the-tank recipes. The focus is on classic Belgian and German styles, but saisons, IPAs and barrel-aged barley wines fill glasses, too.

☆ Entertainment

From the evening-wear elegance of the Lyric Opera to pay-what-you-can storefront theaters and quirky magic lounges, Chicago puts on an impressive slate of performances. Improv laughs and live music spill out of muggy clubs and DIY dive bars nightly. Chicago's spectator sports might just have the most rabid fans of all.

★**Steppenwolf Theatre**   THEATER
(📞312-335-1650; www.steppenwolf.org; 1650 N Halsted St, Lincoln Park; ⊙box office 11am-6:30pm Tue-Sat, from 1pm Sun; Ⓜ Red Line to North/Clybourn) Steppenwolf is Chicago's top stage for quality, provocative theater productions. The Hollywood-heavy ensemble includes Gary Sinise, John Malkovich, Martha Plimpton, Gary Cole, Joan Allen and Tracy Letts. A money-saving tip: the box office releases 20 tickets for $20 for each day's shows; they go on sale at 11am Tuesday to Saturday and at 1pm Sunday, and are available by phone.

iO Theater   COMEDY
(📞312-929-2401; www.ioimprov.com; 1501 N Kingsbury St, Old Town; tickets $5-16; Ⓜ Red Line

to North/Clybourn) One of Chicago's top-tier (and original) improv houses, iO is a bit edgier (and cheaper) than its competition, with four stages hosting bawdy shows of regular and musical improv nightly. Two bars and a beer garden add to the fun. The Improvised Shakespeare Company is awesome; catch them if you can.

Second City
COMEDY

(☎ 312-337-3992; www.secondcity.com; 1616 N Wells St, Lincoln Park; tickets $35-55; Ⓜ Brown, Purple Line to Sedgwick) Bill Murray, Stephen Colbert, Tina Fey and more honed their wit at this slick venue with nightly shows. The Mainstage and ETC stage host sketch revues (with an improv scene thrown in); they're similar in price and quality. If you turn up around 10pm Monday through Thursday (or 1am Saturday or 9pm Sunday) you can watch a free improv set.

Grant Park Orchestra
CLASSICAL MUSIC

(☎ 312-742-7638; www.grantparkmusicfestival. com; Pritzker Pavilion, Millennium Park; ⊘ 6:30pm Wed & Fri, 7:30pm Sat mid-Jun–mid-Aug; Ⓜ Brown, Orange, Green, Purple, Pink Line to Washington/ Wabash) It's a summertime must-do. The Grant Park Orchestra – composed of top-notch musicians from symphonies worldwide – puts on free classical concerts at Millennium Park's Pritzker Pavilion (p77). Patrons bring lawn chairs, blankets, wine and picnic fixings to set the scene as the sun dips, the skyscraper lights flicker on and glorious music fills the night air.

Live Music

★ Green Mill
JAZZ

(☎ 773-878-5552; www.greenmilljazz.com; 4802 N Broadway, Uptown; ⊘ noon-4am Mon-Fri, to 5am Sat, 11am-4am Sun; Ⓜ Red Line to Lawrence) The timeless – and notorious – Green Mill was Al Capone's favorite speakeasy (a trap door behind the bar accessed tunnels for running booze and escaping the feds). Sit in one of the curved booths and feel his ghost urging you on to another martini. Local and national jazz artists perform nightly; on Sunday is the nationally acclaimed poetry slam (www. greenmilljazz.com; 4802 N Broadway, Uptown; cover charge $7; ⊘ 7-10pm Sun; Ⓜ Red Line to Lawrence). Cash only.

★ Buddy Guy's Legends
BLUES

(☎ 312-427-1190; www.buddyguy.com; 700 S Wabash Ave; cover charge Sun-Thu $10, Fri & Sat $20; ⊘ 5pm-2am Mon & Tue, from 11am Wed-Fri,

Berghoff (p89), Chicago
FRANK FELL MEDIA/SHUTTERSTOCK ©

noon-3am Sat, noon-2am Sun; Ⓜ Red Line to Harrison) Top local and national acts wail on the stage of local icon Buddy Guy. The man himself usually plays a series of shows in January; tickets go on sale in October. Free, all-ages acoustic shows are staged at lunch and dinner (the place doubles as a Cajun restaurant); note that you must pay to stay on for late-evening shows.

Old Town School of Folk Music
LIVE MUSIC

(☎ 773-728-6000; www.oldtownschool.org; 4544 N Lincoln Ave, Lincoln Square; 🚻; Ⓜ Brown Line to Western) You can hear the call of the banjos from the street outside this venerable institution, where major national and international acts such as Richard Thompson and Joan Baez play when they come to town. Old Town also hosts superb world-music shows, including every Wednesday at 8:30pm when they're free (or a $10 donation).

Hideout
LIVE MUSIC

(☎ 773-227-4433; www.hideoutchicago.com; 1354 W Wabansia Ave, West Town; tickets $5-15; ⊘ 4pm-midnight Mon-Thu, to 2am Fri, 6pm-3am Sat, hours vary Sun; 🚌 72) Hidden behind a factory past the edge of Bucktown, this two-room lodge of indie rock and alt-country is well worth seeking out. The owners have nursed an outsider, underground vibe, and the place feels like your grandma's rumpus room. Music and other events (talk shows, literary readings, comedy etc) take place nightly. On Mondays there's a great open-mike **poetry night** (www.facebook.com/Weeds-Poetry; by donation; ⊙9:30pm Mon; 🚇9, 72).

Empty Bottle   LIVE MUSIC
(📞773-276-3600; www.emptybottle.com; 1035 N Western Ave, Ukrainian Village; ⊙5pm-2am Mon-Wed, from 3pm Thu & Fri, from 11am Sat & Sun; 🚇49) Chicago's music insiders fawn over the Empty Bottle, the city's scruffy, go-to club for edgy indie rock, jazz and other beats that's been a west-side institution for almost three decades. Monday's show is often a freebie by a couple of up-and-coming bands. Cheap beer, a photo booth and good graffiti-reading in the bathrooms add to the dive-bar fun.

🔒 Shopping

From the glossy stores of the Magnificent Mile to the indie designers of Wicker Park to the brainy booksellers of Hyde Park, Chicago is a shopper's destination. It has been that way from the get-go. After all, this is the city that birthed the department store and traditions such as the money-back guarantee, bridal registry and bargain basement.

⭐ Chicago Architecture
Center Shop   GIFTS & SOUVENIRS
(📞312-922-3432; http://shop.architecture.org; 111 E Wacker Dr; ⊙9am-5pm Mon, Wed & Fri-Sun, to 8pm Tue & Thu; 🚇151, Ⓜ Brown, Orange, Green, Purple, Pink Line to State/Lake) Browse through skyline T-shirts and posters, Frank Lloyd Wright note cards, skyscraper models and heaps of books that celebrate local architecture at this haven for anyone with an edifice complex; a children's section has books to pique the interest of budding builders. The items make excellent 'only in Chicago' souvenirs.

⭐ Reckless Records   MUSIC
(📞773-235-3727; www.reckless.com; 1379 N Milwaukee Ave, Wicker Park; ⊙10am-10pm Mon-Sat, to 8pm Sun; Ⓜ Blue Line to Damen) Chicago's best indie-rock record and CD emporium lets you listen to everything before you buy. There's plenty of elbow room in the big, sunny space, which makes for happy hunting through the new and used bins. DVDs and cassette tapes, too. Stop by for flyers and listing calendars of the local live-music and theater scene.

Gene's Sausage Shop   FOOD & DRINKS
(📞773-728-7243; www.genessausage.com; 4750 N Lincoln Ave, Lincoln Square; ⊙9am-8pm Mon-Sat, to 4pm Sun; Ⓜ Brown Line to Western) As if the hanging sausages, ripe cheeses and flaky pastries lining the shelves at this European market weren't enough, Gene's also rocks a rooftop summer beer garden. Sit at communal picnic tables and munch hot-off-the-grill bratwursts while sipping worldly brews from the tap.

Quimby's   BOOKS
(📞773-342-0910; www.quimbys.com; 1854 W North Ave, Wicker Park; ⊙noon-9pm Mon-Thu, to 10pm Fri, 11am-10pm Sat, noon-7pm Sun; Ⓜ Blue Line to Damen) The epicenter of Chicago's comic and zine worlds, Quimby's is one of the linchpins of underground literary culture in the city. Here you can find everything from crayon-powered punk-rock manifestos to slickly produced graphic novels. It's a groovy place for cheeky literary souvenirs and bizarro readings.

Koval Distillery   DRINKS
(📞312-878-7988; www.koval-distillery.com; 5121 N Ravenswood Ave, Ravenswood; ⊙2-7pm Mon-Fri, 1-6:30pm Sat, 2-5pm Sun; Ⓜ Brown Line to Damen) Koval distills organic, small-batch whiskey and gin in the shiny copper tanks that you see inside. It also makes ginger, jasmine, walnut and other unique liqueurs. The shop in front sells them; you can sample the wares before buying.

The distillery also offers hour-long tours ($10) on Wednesday, Saturday and Sunday, and weekly cocktail classes. The website has the schedule.

ℹ️ Information

Chicago Reader (www.chicagoreader.com) Great listings for music, arts, restaurants and film, plus news and politics.

Choose Chicago (www.choosechicago.com) Official tourism site with sightseeing and event info.

Lonely Planet (www.lonelyplanet.com/chicago) Destination information, hotel reviews and more.

ℹ️ Getting Around

Elevated/subway trains are part of the city's public transportation system. Metra commuter trains venture out into the suburbs.

City buses operate from early morning until late evening. The fare is $2.25 ($2.50 if you want a transfer). You can use a Ventra Card (a rechargeable fare card that you buy at L stations) or pay the driver with exact change. Buses are particularly useful for reaching the Museum Campus, Hyde Park and Lincoln Park's zoo.

GRAND RAPIDS BEER CITY

How did Grand Rapids – a town known for ho-hum office-furniture manufacturing – become hot Beer City? Well, as the manufacturing companies closed up shop over the years, they left behind abandoned industrial buildings – ie cheap space perfect for brewers. There was also a young, thirsty population from the dozen colleges and universities in town.

So people starting cooking up suds. It was pretty under the radar until 2012, when Grand Rapids was voted best beer city in the USA by the national Beer Examiner blog. It happened again in 2013. Then the scene boomed.

Grand Rapids now has around 25 craft breweries in the city proper, and about 20 more in nearby towns. The **Ale Trail** takes you there (download a map at www.experiencegr.com/beer). What makes the scene so popular is the breweries' density – you can walk between many makers – and the relatively low cost of drinking.

The breweries also cater to beer tourists and make it easy to taste the wares. Every taproom offers flights, where you choose the 5oz samples you want to try. Ask at any establishment for the **Brewsader Passport**, a handy little booklet that lists all the beer makers. Collect eight stamps as you make the rounds, and a free Brewsader T-shirt comes your way. You can also download the **Brewsader app** and check in at each brewery you visit.

Top picks in town include Brewery Vivant (p42) for Belgian-style beers in an old chapel, the huge rock-and-roll–style **Founders Brewing Co** (☑616-776-1195; www.foundersbrewing.com; 235 Grandville Ave SW; ⊙11am-2am Mon-Sat, to midnight Sun; 🖥), **Mitten Brewing Company** (☑616-608-5612; www.mittenbrewing.com; 527 Leonard St NW; ⊙11:30am-10pm Sun & Mon, to midnight Tue-Sat) and its wide-ranging brews in a cool old firehouse, and inventive neighborhood gem **Harmony Brewing Company** (☑616-233-0063; www.harmonybeer.com; 1551 Lake Dr SE; ⊙11am-10pm Mon, 11am-midnight Tue-Sat, noon-10pm Sun). These breweries also serve terrific food, which you'll need to stay upright through the evening.

MICHIGAN

More, more, more – Michigan is the Midwest state that cranks it up. It sports more beaches than the Atlantic seaboard. More than half the state is covered by forests. And more cherries and berries get shoveled into pies here than anywhere else in the USA. Plus Detroit is the Midwest's most exciting city of all, reinventing itself daily with street art and fresh architecture.

Michigan occupies prime real estate, surrounded by four of the five Great Lakes – Superior, Michigan, Huron and Erie. Islands – Mackinac, Manitou and Isle Royale – freckle its coast and make top touring destinations. Surf beaches, colored sandstone cliffs and trekkable sand dunes also woo visitors.

The state consists of two parts split by water: the larger Lower Peninsula, shaped like a mitten; and the smaller, lightly populated Upper Peninsula, shaped like a slipper. They are linked by the gasp-worthy Mackinac Bridge, which spans the Straits of Mackinac.

Grand Rapids

POP 200,200

The second-largest city in Michigan, Grand Rapids has gotten its groove on thanks to beer. Around 25 craft breweries operate in town, and suds connoisseurs have been piling in, drawn to their quality, density, proximity to each other and low prices. A foodie scene has built up around the beer makers, and new farm-to-table eateries seem to pop up weekly. Grand Rapids' big-name sculpture park and elegant manors in Heritage Hill intrigue, as well.

⊙ Sights

Frederik Meijer Gardens &
Sculpture Park   GARDENS
(☑616-957-1580; www.meijergardens.org; 1000 E Beltline NE; adult/child $14.50/7; ⊙9am-5pm Mon & Wed-Sat, 9am-9pm Tue, 11am-5pm Sun) The 158-acre gardens feature impressive blooms and hulking works by Auguste Rodin, Henry Moore and others. The sculpture park is star of the show, offering paths and lawns bejeweled with 50 works by artists such as Ai

Weiwei, Claes Oldenburg and Anish Kapoor. The five-story glass conservatory impresses, bursting with tropical plants. The children's garden provides lots to smell, touch and dig into. The tranquil Japanese Garden is another highlight. It is 5 miles east of downtown via I-196.

Gerald R Ford Museum   MUSEUM

(☑ 616-254-0400;   www.fordlibrarymuseum.gov; 303 Pearl St NW; adult/child $10/4; ⊙ 9am-5pm Mon-Sat, from noon Sun) The downtown museum is dedicated to Michigan's only president. Ford stepped into the Oval Office and President Richard Nixon and his vice president, Spiro Agnew, resigned in disgrace. It's a bizarre period in US history, and the museum does an excellent job of covering it, down to displaying the burglary tools used in the Watergate break-in. Ford and wife Betty are buried on the museum's grounds.

☞ Tours

Grand Rapids Beer Tours   FOOD & DRINK

(☑ 616-901-9719; www.grbeertours.com; 250 Grandville Ave SW; 4/6hr tours $55/75) These van tours stop at three or four breweries (depending on tour length). A guide leads you through production facilities and tastings that include four good-sized samples

---

HARBOR COUNTRY

Harbor Country refers to a group of eight small, lake-hugging towns that roll out beaches, wineries, cool shops and all-round rustic charm.

New Buffalo is the largest community, home to a surf school, a busy public beach, ice-cream shops and a beer church. Three Oaks is the only Harbor community that's inland (6 miles in, via Hwy 12). Here Green Acres meets Greenwich Village in a bohemian farm-and-arts blend. Cycle backroads and browse antique stores by day, then visit the cocktail-swirling distillery and folksy theater by night. Union Pier, Lakeside, Harbert and Sawyer are some of the other cutesy towns, chock-full of historic inns, breweries and galleries. Several wineries surround the communities and offer tastings.

For information, see **Harbor Country Chamber of Commerce** (www. harborcountry.org).

---

per venue. Pickup is in front of Grand Rapids' bus station. Tours are limited to 14 people, and they do sell out, so book ahead if possible.

🛏 Sleeping & Eating

CityFlats Hotel   HOTEL $$

(☑ 616-608-1720; www.cityflatshotel.com; 83 Monroe Center St NW; r $175-275; ※ 🛜) 🅿 Rooms at this ecofriendly hotel have big windows for lots of natural light, bamboo linens, cork floors and locally made, reclaimed wood furniture. The building is gold-certified by the Leadership in Energy and Environmental Design (LEED) program. The downtown location puts you near museums, breweries and restaurants.

★ Downtown Market

Grand Rapids   MARKET $

(☑ 616-805-5308; www.downtownmarketgr.com; 435 Ionia Ave SW; baked goods $2-5, mains $10-16; ⊙ 10am-7pm Sun-Thu, 10am-8pm Fri, 9am-8pm Sat; 🛜) Chowhounds hobnob at this stylish food hall, perusing top picks such as Slows Bar BQ, Fish Lads (stellar fish and chips), Love's Ice Cream and Madcap Coffee. The main floor has tables and benches lit by floor-to-ceiling windows, or head upstairs where more tables await, along with a large, veggie-growing greenhouse.

★ Green Well   AMERICAN $$

(☑ 616-808-3566; www.thegreenwell.com; 924 Cherry St SE; mains $15-20; ⊙ 11am-10pm Sun-Tue, to 11pm Wed & Thu, to midnight Fri & Sat) 🅿 Burgers, green curry, and barbecue pork and polenta feature on the menu, where everything is made with sustainably farmed ingredients. Beer plays a role in many dishes, such as the beer-steamed mussels and beer cheese. The bar taps hard-to-find Michigan brews and pours Michigan wines (flights available). Plus, you can buy awesome art by local artists right off the walls.

ℹ Information

Grand Rapids CVB (www.experiencegr.com) Has maps and self-guided brewery tour information online.

Grand Haven

POP 11,070

Grand Haven rocks the classic, old-fashioned beach-town attributes. You know the kind: a waterfront boardwalk, ice-cream shops,

Brewery Vivant (p42), Grand Rapids

sand so clean it squeaks and ooh-and-aah sunsets. The bars and restaurants buzz each evening, and everyone congregates for the eye-popping show by the musical fountain once night falls. Add in the surfing, cycling and inventive breweries, and it's easy to see why Grand Haven blows up each summer.

◉ Sights & Activities

Chinook Pier PIER
(301 N Harbor Dr) Chinook Pier has a lot going on. There's a seasonal mini-golf course (adult/child $3/2) and farmers market (8am to 1pm Wednesday and Saturday). **Wet Mitten Surf Shop** (☑616-844-3388; www.wet mittensurfshop.com; 301 N Harbor Dr, Chinook Pier; ⏱10am-8pm Mon-Sat, 12:30-7pm Sun) and other water-sports outfitters are here. But its biggest claim to fame is its charter fishing fleet. Boats head out to land king salmon and lake trout that occasionally exceed 20 pounds. It's fascinating to be here at the end of the day when the charters return and display their catch.

Musical Fountain FOUNTAIN
(www.ghfountain.com; 101 N Harbor Dr, Waterfront Stadium; ⏱sunset May-Sep) Everyone gathers for the musical fountain performance each evening in summer. It's a trippy tradition to watch water spray high in the sky while synchronized to glowy lights and music. The 25-minute show lets loose nightly in June, July and August, and on Fridays and Satur-

days in May and September. The fountain actually is on the west side of the Grand River, but spectators watch it from Waterfront Stadium's outdoor seats on the east side of the river.

🛏 Sleeping

Boyden House B&B $$
(☑616-846-3538; www.boydenhouse.com; 301 S 5th St; r $120-255; ✳🐾) This rambling Victorian home with gorgeous interior woodwork offers eight rooms that mix antique and modern decor. Some have a private balcony, others have a clawfoot tub or fireplace. All have a comfy featherbed, private bathroom, flat-screen TV and wi-fi. Breakfast is a full cooked extravaganza. It's about a mile walk to the beach.

🍴 Eating & Drinking

Morning Star Café BREAKFAST $
(☑616-844-1131; 711 Washington Ave; mains $6-12; ⏱6:30am-2:30pm) This bright-hued, whimsically decorated cafe cooks the best breakfast in town. The blueberry oatmeal pancakes, pumpkin and cream-cheese crepes, and egg, bacon and cornbread scramble top the list, but there are loads of dishes to choose from, many with a Southwestern bent.

Odd Side Ales MICROBREWERY
(☑616-935-7326; www.oddsideales.com; 41 Washington Ave; ⏱11:30am-11pm Mon-Thu, to midnight Fri & Sat, to 10pm Sun) Odd Side brews some

peculiar experimental suds, like the Mayan Mocha stout (with coffee, cinnamon, nutmeg and habenero chilies) and Aestas sour ale (aged in oak with sea salt, coriander, strawberry and cucumber). The convivial brewpub recently underwent a hefty expansion and now has more than 40 taps delivering the goods.

ℹ Information

Grand Haven CVB (www.visitgrandhaven.com) Provides lodging, activities and events info.

Saugatuck & Douglas

Saugatuck is one of the Gold Coast's most popular resort areas, known for its strong arts community, numerous B&Bs and gay-friendly vibe. Douglas is its twin city a mile or so to the south, and they've pretty much sprawled into one. It's a touristy but funky place, with ice cream–licking families, yuppie boaters and martini-drinking gay couples sharing the waterfront. Galleries and shops fill the compact downtown core. Weekends attract the masses.

Oval Beach   BEACH
(Oval Beach Dr, Saugatuck; ⊙ 9am-10pm) Lifeguards patrol the long expanse of fine sand. There are bathrooms and concession stands, though not enough to spoil the peaceful, dune-laden scene. It costs $10 to park. Or arrive the adventurous way, via chain ferry and a trek over Mt Baldhead.

★**Pines Motorlodge**   MOTEL **$$**
(✓ 269-857-5211; www.thepinesmotorlodge. com; 56 Blue Star Hwy, Douglas; r $139-249; 🖥) Retro-cool tiki lamps, pinewood furniture and communal lawn chairs add up to a fun, social ambience amid the firs in Douglas.

★**Farmhouse Deli**   DELI **$**
(✓ 269-455-5274; www.thefarmhousedeli.com; 100 Blue Star Hwy, Douglas; mains $8-12; ⊙ 9am-6pm; 🖋) 🍽 While it could coast on its looks – the shabby-chic farmhouse decor is cute as a button – the deli ups the ante with seriously top-notch food. The Cubano sandwich (pulled pork, porchetta and Gruyère), tarragon-tinged chicken salad, tangy goat cheeses, cleansing juices and house-baked croissants, cakes and cookies (try the triple ginger molasses one) dazzle.

Virtue Cider   WINERY
(✓ 269-722-3232; www.virtuecider.com; 2170 62nd St, Fennville; ⊙ noon-6pm Tue & Wed, to 7pm Thu-Sun) Head to Virtue's farm in Fennville and sip a pint while sheep bleat, pigs oink and chickens cluck around you. The taproom is in a barrel-strewn barn, where the Brut (crisp and dry) and Percheron (slightly sweet) star among the 13 taps. Flights are available.

WORTH A TRIP

MUSKEGON

The western shore's largest city, Muskegon (population 37,290) features nifty architecture in its downtown district thanks to lumber barons trying to outbuild each other in the late 1800s. Hip taverns, juice bars, bistros and galleries now occupy the structures along Western Ave and its neighboring blocks. **Pigeon Hill Brewing Company** (✓ 231-375-5184; www.pigeonhillbrew.com; 500 W Western Ave, Muskegon; ⊙ noon-10pm Mon-Thu, to midnight Fri & Sat, to 8pm Sun) shows how it's done. Locals hoist pints of eclectic stouts and IPAs in the former garage whose doors slide up to let in fresh air.

Adventure-sports enthusiasts will find action here. The **Muskegon Winter Sports Complex** (✓ 877-879-5843; www.msports.org; 462 Scenic Dr, Muskegon) has one of the nation's only public luge tracks. **Pere Marquette Beach** (Beach Street Rd, Muskegon; ⊙ 6am-11pm) is a hot spot for kiteboarding and paddleboarding, and it hosts the **Great Lakes Surf Festival** (www.greatlakessurffestival.com) in mid-July.

Muskegon is also the departure point for the **Lake Express** (✓ 866-914-1010; www.lake-express.com; 1918 Lakeshore Dr, Muskegon; one way adult/child/car $96/39/105; ⊙ May-Oct) ferry that glides to Milwaukee, WI. **Shoreline Inn** (✓ 231-727-8483; www.shorelineinn. com; 750 Terrace Point Rd, Muskegon; r $120-190; 🅿 🕸 🛜 📶) provides waterfront lodging if you need a place to crash before or after your boat ride.

The city is 15 miles north of Grand Haven on US 31. See www.visitmuskegon.org for more information.

ℹ️ Information

Saugatuck/Douglas CVB (www.saugatuck.com) Provides foodie, family and LGBTIQ+ focused trip-planning info.

Sleeping Bear Dunes National Lakeshore

Eye-popping lake views from atop colossal sand dunes? Water blue enough to be in the Caribbean? Miles of unspoiled beaches? Secluded islands with mystical trees? All here at Sleeping Bear Dunes, along with lush forests, terrific day hikes and glass-clear waterways for paddling. The national park stretches from north of Frankfort to just before Leland, on the Leelanau Peninsula. Several cute little towns fringe the area.

👁 Sights & Activities

Manitou Islands ISLAND
(per family $25) The forest-cloaked Manitou Islands provide an off-the-beaten-path adventure. They're part of Sleeping Bear Dunes National Lakeshore, hence the entrance fee. North Manitou is known for star-speckled backcountry camping, while South Manitou is terrific for wilderness-rich day trips. Kayaking and hiking are the big to-dos, especially the 7-mile trek to the Valley of the Giants, an otherworldly stand of cedar trees on South Manitou. Manitou Island Transit (p43) runs ferries from Leland; the trip takes 1½ hours.

Dune Climb HIKING
(Hwy 109, Glen Arbor; ⏰24hr) The Dune Climb is the park's most popular attraction, where you trudge up a 200ft-high dune and then run or roll down. Gluttons for leg-muscle punishment can keep slogging all the way to Lake Michigan, a strenuous 1½-hour trek one way; bring water. The site, with a parking lot and bathrooms, is on Hwy 109, 5 miles north of Empire.

Sleeping Bear Heritage Trail CYCLING
(www.sleepingbeartrail.org; Empire) The 22-mile paved path goes from Empire to Bohemian Rd (aka County Rd 669), passing dreamy forested areas, quaint towns and the Dune Climb along the way; walkers and cyclists are all over it. For the most part it rolls gently up and down, though there are some larger hills at the southern end. Trailheads with parking lots are located roughly every 3 miles; the one at Bar Lake Rd, near Empire, is a good place to embark.

🛏 Sleeping & Eating

Glen Arbor B&B B&B $$
(☎231-334-6789; www.glenarborlodging.com; 6548 Western Ave, Glen Arbor; r $155-290, without bath $115-160; ⏰closed mid-Nov–Apr) The owners renovated this century-old farmhouse into a sunny, French country inn with six themed rooms.

Empire Village Inn AMERICAN $
(☎231-326-5101; www.empirevillageinn.com; 11601 S Lacore Rd, Empire; mains $10-17; ⏰noon-10pm) Enter the low A-frame building, grab a seat at a scuffed wood table and order one of the local beers on tap while waiting for your excellent, doughy-crust pizza to arrive. Burgers and sandwiches satisfy too, along with the housemade root beer. It's a swell place to refuel after a day of hiking or biking, if you don't mind the noisy hubbub.

🍺 Drinking

Stormcloud Brewing Company MICROBREWERY
(☎231-352-0118; www.stormcloudbrewing.com; 303 Main St, Frankfort; ⏰11:30am-10pm Sun-Thu, to 11pm Fri & Sat) Belgian-style beers are Stormcloud's gift to the universe. Rainmaker Ale is its medal winner (bronze at the Great American Beer Festival), and there are 15 other taps of unusual and sometimes fruity brews. They're terrific paired with the flatbread pizzas and sharable plates such as smoked whitefish spread on toast. Gluten-free and vegan options are available.

ℹ️ Information

Sleeping Bear Dunes National Lakeshore Visitor Center (p42) has information, trail maps and vehicle entry permits.

Traverse City

15,700

Michigan's 'cherry capital' is the largest city in the northern half of the Lower Peninsula. It's got a bit of urban sprawl, but it's still a happenin' base from which to see the Sleeping Bear Dunes, Mission Peninsula wineries, U-pick orchards and other area attractions. The food and arts scenes are superb, comparable to those of a much larger urban area.

HEMMINGWAY'S HAUNTS

A number of writers have ties to northwest Michigan, but none are as famous as Ernest Hemingway, who spent the summers of his youth at his family's cottage on Walloon Lake. Hemingway buffs often tour the area to view the places that made their way into his writing.

Horton Bay General Store (p44) A short distance north of Charlevoix, Boyne City Rd veers off to the east. It skirts Lake Charlevoix and eventually arrives at Horton Bay. Hemingway fans will recognize the store, with its 'high false front,' from his short story 'Up in Michigan.' The old-time shop now sells groceries, souvenirs, sandwiches and ice cream, plus wine and tapas on weekend nights (reservations required for the latter).

Little Traverse Historical Museum (p44) Further north on US 31, stop in Petoskey to see the museum's Hemingway collection, including rare first-edition books that the author autographed for a friend when he visited in 1947.

City Park Grill (p44) A few blocks from the museum, toss back a drink at this bar where Hemingway was a regular.

Tour Hemingway's Michigan (www.mihemingwaytour.com) provides further information for self-guided jaunts.

Road-tripping out to the wineries is a must. Head north from Traverse City on Hwy 37 for 20 miles to the end of the grape- and cherry-planted Old Mission Peninsula. You'll be spoiled for choice. The wineries stay open all year round, with reduced hours in winter.

Brys Estate Vineyard & Winery WINERY
(☑ 231-223-9303; www.brysestate.com; 3309 Blue Water Rd; ☺ 11am-7pm Mon-Sat, to 6pm Sun late May-early Sep, reduced hours rest of year) Michigan's excellent wines taste even better on Brys Estate's sprawling deck, which provides stunning vineyard and bay views. Tastings from $8; cheese and charcuterie plates available.

Paddle TC WATER SPORTS
(☑ 231-492-0223; www.paddletc.com; 111 E Grandview Pkwy, Clinch Park; kayaks per hr from $30, tours from $45; ☺ 9am-9pm May-Oct) Offers bike, kayak and stand-up-paddleboard rentals, starting at $30 per hour. Tours and lessons available; the KaBrew tour ($69), a kayak and bike crawl of local craft breweries, is highly recommended. Call for times.

Island View Cottages COTTAGE $$
(☑ 231-947-2863; www.islandv.com; 853 E Front St; cottages $125-250; ❄ 🐾) Island View's tidy property features nine cottages and three houses that front a private beach. The grounds have fire pits, grills, and basketball and shuffleboard courts. It's located a half-mile walk from downtown's eating and drinking core. Bookings go through Airbnb.

★ **Filling Station** PIZZA $
(☑ 231-946-8168; www.thefillingstationmicro brewery.com; 642 Railroad Pl; mains $10-16; ☺ 11am-11pm Mon-Thu, to midnight Fri & Sat, noon-10pm Sun) This family-owned business in a former railway terminal has been serving up wood-fired pizzas, fresh green salads and craft beer since 2012. Check out the specials board for seasonal items such as the Oktoberfest pizza, with brats, sauerkraut and a mustard crème fraîche. A s'mores dessert pizza is a sweet ending.

★ **Short's Production Facility Pull Barn** BREWERY
(☑ 231-498-2300; www.shortsbrewing.com; 211 Industrial Park Dr; ☺ noon-8pm Mon-Fri, 11am-9pm Sat & Sun late May-early Sep) Beer buffs adore Short's for its Huma Lupa Licious IPA and Juicy Brut ale, and they come en masse to this sprawling outdoor drinking yard in Elk Rapids (18 miles northeast of Traverse City) to get their fill. Folks settle in at shaded picnic tables, play bean-bag toss games and while away the afternoon gulping brews from the 15 on tap.

❶ Information

Traverse City Tourism (www.traversecity.com)

Charlevoix & Petoskey

These two towns, among the most affluent along Michigan's western shore, brim with yacht-filled marinas and fancy summer homes. They're not snooty though, and they provide a fair bit of offbeat adventure. Beachcombing, island trekking and following in the footsteps of Ernest Hemingway await those who make the trip.

★ **Stafford's Perry Hotel**   HOTEL $$
(☑231-347-4000; www.theperryhotel.com; 100 Lewis St, Petoskey; r $169-299; ❀@☎) The Perry Hotel is a grand historic place. Hemingway once stayed here (in 1916 after a hiking and camping trip in the region). Count on comfy beds, vintage furniture and a cozy onsite pub. Pricier rooms have bay views.

★ **Beards Brewery**   MICROBREWERY
(☑231-753-2221; www.beardsbrewery.com; 215 E Lake St, Petoskey; ⊙11:30am-10pm Tue-Thu, 11:30am-11pm Fri, 10am-11pm Sat, 11;30am-9pm Sun) A couple of hairy-faced home brewers got together to open Beards, and they know their stuff, as the hoppy IPAs, tart saisons and nutty brown ales flowing from the 20 taps attest. It's a community gathering spot hosting trivia nights and local musicians. The awesome outdoor patio overlooks the bay, and a fire pit keeps you toasty on cool nights.

Straits of Mackinac

This region, between the Upper and Lower Peninsulas, features a long history of forts and fudge shops. Car-free Mackinac Island is Michigan's premier tourist draw.

One of the most spectacular sights in the area is the 5-mile-long Mackinac Bridge (known locally as 'Big Mac'), which spans the Straits of Mackinac. The $4 toll is worth every penny as the views from the bridge, which include two Great Lakes, two peninsulas and hundreds of islands, are second to none in Michigan.

And remember: despite the spelling, it's pronounced *mac*-in-aw.

Mackinaw City

POP 795

At the south end of Mackinac Bridge, bordering I-75, is touristy Mackinaw City. It serves mainly as a jumping-off point to Mackinac Island, but it does have a couple of intriguing historic sights.

Colonial Michilimackinac   HISTORIC SITE
(☑231-436-5564; www.mackinacparks.com; 102 W Straits Ave; adult/child $12.50/7.25; ⊙9am-7pm Jun-Aug, to 5pm May & Sep-early Oct; ⊞) Next to the Big Mac bridge (its visitor center is actually beneath the bridge) is Colonial Michilimackinac, a National Historic Landmark that features a reconstructed stockade first built in 1715 by the French. Costumed interpreters cook and craft here.

Mackinac Island

From either Mackinaw City or St Ignace, you can catch a ferry to Mackinac Island. The island's location in the straits between Lake Michigan and Lake Huron made it a prized port in the North American fur trade, and a site the British and Americans battled over many times.

The most important date on this 3.8-sq-mile island was 1898 – the year cars were banned in order to encourage tourism. Today all travel is by horse or bicycle; even the police use bikes to patrol the town. The crowds of tourists – called Fudgies by the islanders – can be crushing at times, particularly during summer weekends. But when the last ferry leaves in the evening and clears out the day-trippers, Mackinac's real charm emerges and you drift back into another, slower era.

Eighty percent of the island is state parkland. Not much stays open between November and April.

Arch Rock   NATURAL FEATURE
FREE This huge limestone arch curves 150ft above Lake Huron and provides dramatic

Arch Rock, Mackinac Island
SUSAN MONTGOMERY/SHUTTERSTOCK ©

photo opportunities. You can get here two ways: from stairs that lead up from the lakeshore road, or from the island's interior via Arch Rock Rd. The site crowds with tour groups around midday, so try visiting early in the morning.

Fort Mackinac   HISTORIC SITE
(☑906-847-3328; www.mackinacparks.com; 7127 Huron Rd; adult/child $13.50/8; ⊙9:30am-7pm Jun-Aug, reduced hours May & Sep–mid-Oct, closed mid-Oct–Apr; ◉) Fort Mackinac sits atop limestone cliffs near downtown. Built by the British in 1780, it's one of the best-preserved military forts in the country. Costumed interpreters and cannon and rifle firings (every half-hour) entertain the kids. Stop at the tearoom for a bite and a million-dollar view of downtown and the Straits of Mackinac from the outdoor tables.

① Information

Mackinac Island Visitor Center (☑906-847-3783; www.mackinacisland.org; 7274 Main St; ⊙9am-5pm May-Oct) Downtown booth with maps for hiking and cycling.

MINNESOTA

Is Minnesota really the land of 10,000 lakes, as it's so often advertised? You betcha! Actually, in typically modest style, the state has undermarketed itself – there are 11,842 lakes. Which is great news for travelers. Intrepid outdoors folk can wet their paddles in the Boundary Waters, where nighttime brings a blanket of stars and the lullaby of wolf howls. Those wanting to get further off the beaten

path can journey to Voyageurs National Park, where there's more water than roadway. If that all seems too far-flung, stick to the Twin Cities of Minneapolis and St Paul, where you can't swing a moose without hitting something cool or cultural. And for those looking for middle ground – a cross between the big city and big woods – the dramatic, freighter-filled port of Duluth beckons.

① Information

Minnesota Highway Conditions (www.511mn.org) Handy for checking winter road conditions before heading out.

Minnesota Office of Tourism (www.explore minnesota.com) Official Minnesota travel portal.

Minnesota State Park Information (☑reservations 866-857-2757; www.dnr.state.mn.us) Park entry requires a vehicle permit (per day/year $7/35). Tent and RV sites cost $15 to $31; reservations accepted for a $7 fee online, $10 by phone.

Minneapolis

POP 422,300

Minneapolis is the biggest and artsiest town on the prairie, with all the trimmings of progressive prosperity – swank art museums, rowdy rock clubs, organic and ethnic eateries, and edgy theaters. It's always happenin', even in winter. And here's the bonus: folks are attitude-free and the embodiment of 'Minnesota Nice.' Count how many times they tell you to 'Have a great day,' come rain, shine or snow.

The city owes its existence to the Mississippi. Water-powered sawmills along the river fueled a boom in timber in the mid-1800s. Wheat from the prairies also needed to be processed, so flour mills churned into the next big business. The population grew rapidly in the late 19th century with mass immigration, especially from Scandinavia and Germany. There has been a more recent wave of immigration in the past few decades, from places such as Vietnam and Somalia.

◉ Sights & Activities

★**Walker Art Center**   MUSEUM
(☑612-375-7600; www.walkerart.org; 1750 Hennepin Ave; adult/child $15/free; ⊙11am-5pm Tue, Wed & Sun, to 9pm Thu, to 6pm Fri & Sat) The first-class art center has a strong permanent collection of 20th-century art and photography, including big-name US painters and great US pop art. On Monday evenings from

late July to late August, the museum hosts free movies and music across the pedestrian bridge in Loring Park that are quite the to-do.

★ **Minneapolis Sculpture Garden** GARDENS (www.walkerart.org/visit/garden; 725 Vineland Pl; ⊙6am-midnight) FREE This 19-acre green space, studded with contemporary works such as the oft-photographed *Spoonbridge and Cherry* by Claes Oldenburg, sits beside the Walker Art Center. The Cowles Conservatory, abloom with exotic hothouse flowers, is also on the grounds. In summer (May to September) a trippy mini-golf course (adult/child $10/8) amid the sculptures adds to the fun.

Endless Bridge OBSERVATORY (Guthrie Theater; 818 2nd St S; ⊙8am-8pm, to 11pm performance days) FREE Head inside the cobalt-blue Guthrie Theater and make your way up the escalator to the Endless Bridge, a far-out cantilevered walkway overlooking the Mississippi River. You don't need a theater ticket, as it's intended as a public space. The theater's 9th-floor Amber Box provides another knockout view.

Weisman Art Museum MUSEUM (☑612-625-9494; www.wam.umn.edu; 333 E River Parkway; ⊙10am-5pm Tue, Thu & Fri, to 8pm Wed, 11am-5pm Sat & Sun) FREE The Weisman, which occupies a swooping silver structure by architect Frank Gehry, is a university (and city) highlight. The airy main galleries hold cool collections of 20th-century American art, ceramics, Korean furniture and works on paper.

Minneapolis Institute of Art MUSEUM (☑612-870-3000; https://new.artsmia.org; 2400 3rd Ave S; ⊙10am-5pm Tue, Wed & Sat, 10am-9pm Thu & Fri, 11am-5pm Sun) FREE This museum is a huge trove housing a veritable history of art. The modern and contemporary collections will astonish, while the Asian galleries (2nd floor) and Decorative Arts rooms (3rd floor) are also highlights. Allot at least a few hours to visit. The museum is a mile south of downtown via 3rd Ave S.

🎊 Festivals & Events

Twin Cities Pride LGBT (www.tcpride.org; 1382 Willow St, Loring Park; ⊙mid-Jun) One of the USA's largest, the Twin Cities Pride Festival draws more than 300,000 revelers to Loring Park.

🛏 Sleeping & Eating

Aloft HOTEL $$ (☑612-455-8400; www.marriott.com; 900 Washington Ave S; r $159-265; P❄@🛜🏊) Aloft's efficiently designed, industrial-toned rooms draw a younger clientele. The clubby lobby has board games, a cocktail lounge and 24-hour snacks. There's a tiny pool, a decent fitness room and a bike-share station outside the front door. Parking costs $25.

Hewing Hotel HOTEL $$ (☑651-468-0400; www.hewinghotel.com; 300 Washington Ave N; r $140-260; P❄🛜🏊🐕) This North Loop stunner offers 124 rooms spread through a century-old farm-machine warehouse. The vibe is rustic and cozy. The handsome chambers feature wood-beam ceilings, exposed brick walls and distinctive outdoorsy decor, such as deer-print wallpaper and plaid wool blankets. It's within walking distance of downtown's action (plus there's a bar-restaurant on-site). Parking costs $46.

My Huong VIETNAMESE $ (☑612-702-2922; www.myhuongkitchen.com; 2718 Nicollet Ave S; mains $10-14; ⊙11am-9pm Tue-Sat, to 6pm Sun; 🐕) A modest Vietnamese restaurant turning out authentic versions of banh mi, pho, rolls and lemongrass dishes to an appreciative 'Eat Street' public. The dining room is tiny, but don't let that dissuade you from arguably the best Vietnamese food in the area.

★ **Young Joni** PIZZA $$ (☑612-345-5719; www.youngjoni.com; 165 13th Ave NE; mains $14-19; ⊙4-11pm Tue-Thu, to midnight Fri, noon-midnight Sat, to 10pm Sun) Young Joni fuses two seemingly unrelated types: pizza and Korean food. Here, you can order a wood-fired, crisp-crusted prosciutto, gruyere and ricotta pie with a side of spicy clams, kimchi and tofu. It sounds odd, but the dishes are terrific. Bonus: the hip, industrial space has a hidden bar in back. If the red light is on, the cocktails are flowing.

Twin Cities Pride (p101), Minneapolis

🍷 Drinking & Nightlife

Minneapolis is all in on the local brewing trend, and most makers have taprooms.

★ LynLake Brewery BREWERY
(☑612-224-9682; www.lynlakebrewery.com; 2934 Lyndale Ave S; ⊙5-10pm Mon-Thu, 5pm-1am Fri, noon-1am Sat, noon-10pm Sun; 🛜) The inventive brewers at this popular Uptown micro-brewery and taproom have hit on the right mix of beers (everything from sweet stouts to piney-flavored hop bombs) to location (a former theater, with vast interior drinking spaces and an inviting rooftop terrace). It gets very crowded on Friday and Saturday nights.

Surly Brewing BREWERY
(☑763-999-4040; www.surlybrewing.com; 520 Malcolm Ave SE; ⊙11am-11pm Sun-Thu, to midnight Fri & Sat; 🛜; ⓡgreen) Surly's sprawling, mod-industrial, family-friendly beer hall is mobbed by locals who come for the 20 rotating taps and abundant meaty snacks. Try CynicAle, a Belgian-style saison, or Furious, the flagship American IPA. The destination brewery is in the Prospect Park neighborhood, next to the University of Minnesota. It's a short walk from the Prospect Park Green Line station.

Wilde Cafe CAFE
(☑612-331-4544; www.wildecafe.com; 65 Main St SE; ⊙7am-9pm Sun-Thu, to 11pm Fri & Sat; 🛜) This cafe features amazing baked goods, riverfront digs and a Victorian ambience worthy of its namesake, Oscar Wilde.

Gay Nineties CLUB
(☑612-333-7755; www.gay90s.com; 408 Hennepin Ave; cover $5-10; ⊙8am-2am Mon-Sat, from 10am Sun; 🛜) This long-standing club has dancing, dining and drag shows that attract both a gay and straight clientele.

☆ Entertainment

First Avenue & 7th St Entry LIVE MUSIC
(☑612-332-1775; www.first-avenue.com; 701 1st Ave N; shows from $20) This is the long-standing bedrock of Minneapolis' music scene. First Avenue is the main room featuring national acts; smaller 7th St Entry is for up-and-comers. Check out the exterior stars on the building: they're all bands that have graced the stage. Buy tickets via the website.

Guthrie Theater THEATER
(☑612-377-2224; www.guthrietheater.org; 818 2nd St S; shows $30-90; ⊙box office 11am-5pm) This is Minneapolis's top-gun theater troupe, with a jumbo facility to prove it. Unsold 'rush' tickets go on sale 30 minutes before showtime for $15 to $35 (cash only). Download free audio tours from the website for self-guided jaunts around the funky building.

Target Field BASEBALL
(☑ 800-338-9467; www.mlb.com/twins; 353 N 5th St; ᖆ blue, green) This downtown stadium is home field for Major League Baseball's Minnesota Twins. The season runs from April through October (that is, if the Twins play well enough to make it into October). The stadium is notable for its beyond-the-norm, locally focused food and drink.

US Bank Stadium SPECTATOR SPORT
(☑ 612-338-4537; www.vikings.com; 900 5th St S; ᖆ; ᖆ blue, green) The National Football League's Minnesota Vikings play at this spiffy, glass-walled indoor arena on Sundays from September through December. See the website for a game schedule. Buy tickets online.

🛍 Shopping

★ **Electric Fetus** MUSIC
(☑ 612-870-9300; www.electricfetus.com; 2000 4th Ave S; ⊙ 9am-9pm Mon-Fri, 9am-8pm Sat, 11am-6pm Sun) This indie record store sells a whopping selection of new and used CDs and vinyl, plus groovy hats, T-shirts and incense. It has the lowdown on the local music scene, complete with concert tickets for sale (check the whiteboard behind the counter). Prince used to come here to browse, and the store stocks a good selection of his tunes.

Mall of America MALL
(☑ 952-883-8800; www.mallofamerica.com; off I-494 at 24th Ave; ⊙ 10am-9:30pm Mon-Sat, 11am-7pm Sun; ᖆ; ᖆ blue) Welcome to the USA's largest shopping center. Yes, it's just a mall, filled with the usual stores, movie theaters and eateries. But there's also a wedding chapel inside. And an 18-hole mini-golf course (☑ 952-883-8777; 3rd fl; per person $12; ⊙ 10am-9:30pm Mon-Sat, 11am-7pm Sun). And a zipline. And an amusement park, aka **Nickelodeon Universe** (www. nickelodeonuniverse.com; ⊙ 10am-9:30pm Mon-Sat, 11am-7pm Sun), with 28 rides, including a couple of scream-inducing roller coasters. To walk through will cost you nothing; a one-day, unlimited-ride wristband is $37; or you can pay for rides individually ($3.60 to $7.20).

ⓘ Information

Minneapolis Visitor Information (☑ 612-397-9278; www.minneapolis.org; 505 Nicollet Mall, Suite 100; ⊙ 9am-6pm Mon-Fri, to 5pm Sat, to 3pm Sun; ᖆ) The staff at this downtown

tourist office will bend over backwards to help you set up an itinerary, sort out transportation or find a place to eat or drink. In addition to the copious brochures and maps, there's also an on-site souvenir and gift shop.

St Paul
POP 306,600

St Paul, Minnesota's capital city, is smaller and quieter than its twin to the west, Minneapolis. While Minneapolis is all glitz and bustle, St Paul is more prim and proper and has managed to retain more of its historic character. St Paul's amenities are more modest as well, though the capital does excel when it comes to breweries and brew pubs. The city is well worth a day's diversion from Minneapolis to stroll through the historic residential areas southwest of downtown, particularly along Summit Ave, or closer to the Mississippi River around Irvine Park, to gawk at the late-19th- and early-20th-century mansions. This is also F Scott Fitzgerald's old stomping grounds, and the house he was born in as well as the house where he lived when he published *This Side of Paradise* are still standing.

◉ Sights & Activities

Landmark Center MUSEUM
(☑ 651-292-3225; www.landmarkcenter.org; 75 W 5th St; ⊙ 8am-5pm Mon-Fri, 8am-8pm Thu, 10am-5pm Sat, noon-5pm Sun) Downtown's turreted 1902 Landmark Center used to be the federal courthouse, where gangsters such as Alvin 'Creepy' Karpis were tried; plaques next to the various rooms show who was brought to justice here. In addition to the city's visitor center, the building also contains a couple of small museums (one focusing on wood art, another on music).

Down In History Tours WALKING
(☑ 651-292-1220; www.wabashastreetcaves.com; 215 S Wabasha St; tours $9-10; ⊙ 4pm Mon, 5pm Thu, 11am Sat & Sun May-Sep) These 45-minute tours explore St Paul's underground caves, which gangsters once used as a speakeasy. The fun ramps up on Thursday nights, when a swing band plays in the caverns (additional $8).

🎉 Festivals & Events

St Paul Winter Carnival CULTURAL
(www.wintercarnival.com; ⊙ late Jan-early Feb) Ten days of ice sculptures, ice-skating and ice fishing. Events take place at Rice Park and other venues around the city.

DULUTH TRAVERSE

A 40-mile mountain-bike trail that spans the city and surrounding area? Riders are stoked for the Duluth Traverse (www.coggs.com), a single-track path that's opening bit by bit and linking several existing trails. When it's finished, no Duluth resident will be more than a few minutes from the route. Runners, hikers and snowshoers can also commune with the pines along the way.

📖 Sleeping & Eating

★ Hotel 340   BOUTIQUE HOTEL $$

(☑651-280-4120; www.hotel340.com; 340 Cedar St; r $109-199; P❋@☎) Hotel 340 delivers old-world ambience aplenty, and it's usually a great deal to boot. The 56 rooms in the stately old building have hardwood floors and plush linens. The two-story lobby stokes a grand fireplace and a nifty little bar (the desk staff double as bartenders). Parking costs $17 per night.

Covington Inn   B&B $$

(☑651-292-1411; www.covingtoninn.com; 100 Harriet Island Rd; r $170-265; P❋☎) This four-room, Harriet Island B&B is on a tugboat floating in the Mississippi River; watch the river traffic glide by while sipping your morning coffee. The stately rooms have bright splashes of color, and each has a gas fireplace to keep you toasty in winter.

★ Keg & Case   FOOD HALL $

(☑651-443-6060; www.kegandcase.com; 928 7th St W; sandwiches $12-15; ☉6:30am-10pm Sun-Fri, to midnight Sat; ☎♪) 🍴 A scrumptious food hall, with stalls serving locally sourced sandwiches, pizza, ice cream and other food items in a spiffy, remodeled brewery space. In addition to food vendors, there are stalls where you can purchase mushrooms, condiments, jellies and gifts. It's well worth the trip south of downtown. There are plenty of vegetarian options.

Cook   AMERICAN $

(☑651-756-1787; www.cookstp.com; 1124 Payne Ave; mains $10-15; ☉7am-2pm Mon, Thu & Fri, 7am-3pm Sat & Sun) This cute, sunny spot serves creative diner dishes (gingery French toast, curried veggie burgers, braised short-rib sandwiches), including some with a spicy Korean twist. Cook also hosts Korean dinners on Friday nights. It's located in the burgeoning East Side neighborhood, where several other foodie hot spots are sprouting on Payne Ave.

🍷 Drinking & Entertainment

Summit Brewing Company   BREWERY

(☑651-265-7800; www.summitbrewing.com; 910 Montreal Circle; ☉2-9pm Thu & Fri, noon-9pm Sat, to 6pm Sun) While Summit is one of the state's largest brewers, its beer hall is welcomingly low-key. Inside it's a big open space with communal tables, large windows and around 14 beers on tap. Outside there's a patio that overlooks the river bluffs. Try the Keller pils, oatmeal stout or anything in the experimental Unchained series. Everything is really reasonably priced.

Allianz Field   SPECTATOR SPORT

(www.mnufc.com; 400 Snelling Ave N) The gleaming home field of Minnesota United FC of the North American Soccer League opened its doors in 2019. See the website for a current schedule. Buy tickets online.

Fitzgerald Theater   THEATER

(☑651-290-1200; www.thefitzgeraldtheater.com; 10 E Exchange St) This atmospheric theater hosts big-name musicians, comedians and authors in association with Minnesota Public Radio. See the website for a list of events and ticket information.

ⓘ Information

Mississippi River Visitor Center (☑651-293-0200; www.nps.gov/miss; 120 W Kellogg Blvd; ☉9:30am-5pm Sun & Tue-Thu, to 9pm Fri & Sat) Operated by the National Park Service, it occupies an alcove in the science museum lobby. Stop by to pick up trail maps and see what sort of free ranger-guided activities are going on. In summer these include short hikes to the river and bicycle rides. In winter, there are ice-fishing and snowshoeing jaunts.

St Paul Visitor Center (☑651-292-3225; www.visitsaintpaul.com; 75 W 5th St; ☉10am-4pm Mon-Sat, from noon Sun) In the Landmark Center, it makes a good first stop for maps and DIY walking-tour info.

Northern Minnesota

Northern Minnesota is a veritable outdoor playground. The immense Boundary Waters wilderness is the main draw, and from May through September, kayaks and canoes ply the state's many fabled lakes, though the area is big enough to still feel as if you have the place to yourself. The red-cliffed Lake Superior shoreline and watery Voyageurs National Park are also popular seasonal destinations.

The north has a compelling heritage story to tell as well. For decades the region's biggest city and port, Duluth, shipped the iron ore that fueled mills throughout the Midwest. You can see the old ships and catch some of the city's revivalist spirit, this time centered around craft beer. The old mining town of Hibbing, at the heart of the Iron Range District, is home to an iron-ore mine so vast, it's referred to as Minnesota's 'Grand Canyon.'

Duluth

POP 86,300

Duluth is a brawny shot-and-a-beer port town that offers visitors a glimpse into its storied history as a major shipping center, as well as some citified cultural, dining and drinking amenities. Duluth grew wealthy throughout most of the 20th century as a major exporter of high-quality iron ore, which was carted away on vast ships over the Great Lakes to factories and mills in Michigan, Indiana and Ohio. The port suffered in the 1970s and '80s, though, as the mills shut and the ore reserves dried up.

Shipping is still a major industry, but officials have now turned to tourism to supplement the local economy. You'll find a smattering of interesting sights near the port centered on Duluth's industrial past as well as a burgeoning adventure-sports scene. The downtown is rejuvenating rapidly and there's a fun craft-beer and cider subculture developing on the formerly seedy streets, west of the downtown.

◉ Sights & Activities

Aerial Lift Bridge   BRIDGE
See p48.

Maritime Visitor Center   MUSEUM
(☑ 218-720-5260; www.lsmma.com; 600 Canal Park Dr; ⊙10am-9pm Jun-Aug, reduced hours Sep-May) FREE Located next to the Aerial Lift Bridge, the center has computer screens inside that tell what time the big ships will be sailing through. Cool model boats and exhibits on Great Lakes shipwrecks also make it a top stop in town.

Bob Dylan's Birthplace   NOTABLE BUILDING
(519 N 3rd Ave E) While the town of Hibbing and the Iron Range are most often associated with Bob Dylan, he was born in Duluth in 1941. You'll see brown-and-white signs on Superior St and London Rd for **Bob Dylan Way** (www.bobdylanway.com), pointing out places associated with the legend (like the armory where he saw Buddy Holly in concert, and decided to become a musician). But you're on your own to find Dylan's birthplace, up a hill a few blocks northeast of downtown. Dylan lived on the top floor until age six, when his family moved inland to Hibbing. It's a private residence (and unmarked), so all you can do is stare from the street.

Duluth Experience   ADVENTURE
(☑ 218-464-6337; www.theduluthexperience.com; tours from $79) This outfit offers a range of kayaking, cycling and brewery tours; gear and transportation are provided. Most jaunts depart from Fitger's.

🛏 Sleeping & Eating

Park Point Marina Inn   HOTEL $$
(☑ 218-491-7111; www.parkpointmarinainn.com; 1033 Minnesota Ave; r $135-275; P❄@🛜🏊) This immaculate property is located south of the Aerial Lift Bridge on the point that juts out into Lake Superior. Don't expect luxury, but rather tidy, well-maintained rooms and public areas, and a clean pool

Aerial Lift Bridge, Duluth
NORIHISA TAGUCHI/SHUTTERSTOCK ©

Split Rock Lighthouse

for the kids. The attractions around Canal Park are 10 minutes' walk away, but you'll need your own wheels to get much further than that.

★ **OMC Smokehouse**   BARBECUE $$
(☑ 218-606-1611;   www.omcsmokehouse.com; 1909 W Superior St; mains $15-30; ⊙ 11am-9pm Sun-Thu, to 10pm Fri & Sat) The 'OMC' stands for 'Oink, Moo, Cluck,' but we'll give them a pass because of the outstanding quality of the smoked meats, as well as inventive menu items such as catfish tacos and pork 'n' grits. For drinks, there's a strong lineup of local craft brews from Bent Paddle and Castle Danger. Find it in the Lincoln Park Craft District.

New Scenic Cafe   AMERICAN $$$
(☑ 218-525-6274; www.newsceniccafe.com; 5461 North Shore Dr; sandwiches $15-17, mains $26-35; ⊙ 11am-9pm Sun-Thu, to 10pm Fri & Sat) ♥ Foodies travel from far and near to New Scenic Cafe, 8 miles beyond Duluth on Old Hwy 61. There, in a humble wood-paneled room, they fork into rustic salmon with creamed leeks or a slice of triple berry pie, all served with a generous helping of lake views. Make reservations.

🍷 Drinking & Entertainment

Duluth Cider   BAR
(☑ 218-464-1111; www.duluthcider.com; 2307 W Superior St; ⊙ noon-10pm Mon-Thu, to 11pm Fri & Sat, to 8pm Sun; 🛜) This cider-maker and

taproom, in the Lincoln Park Craft District, was hived from an old livery for the Duluth post office. You'll find a creative menu of apple-based hard ciders, including varieties infused with tequila-oak, orange and strawberry.

Norshor Theatre   THEATER
(☑ 218-733-7555; www.norshortheatre.com; 211 E Superior St) Standing at the center of the city's efforts to revitalize the central business district, this landmark's offerings vary from standard theater to concert performances and screenings of classic films. Check the website.

ℹ Information

Duluth Visitors Center (☑ 800-438-5884; www.visitduluth.com; 21 W Superior St; ⊙ 8:30am-5pm Mon-Fri) Pick up a visitor guide; the website has deals and coupons.

North Shore

A trip here is dominated by water – mainly enormous, tempestuous Lake Superior – where ore-toting freighters ply the ports, little fishing fleets haul in the day's catch and wave-bashed cliffs offer awesome views if you're willing to trek. Numerous river valleys, waterfalls, hiking trails and little towns speckle the landscape as it unfurls to the Canadian border.

The highlights along the shoreline highway that leads north from Duluth include a series of state parks that offer their own unique delights. You'll find twisting gorges and dramatic waterfalls at Gooseberry Falls, Judge CR Magney and Temperance River state parks. A lonely lighthouse beckons at Split Rock, not far from Two Harbors. The picturesque artistic retreat at Grand Marais, with its relatively 'big city' amenities such as good food and drink, caps off the drive. The town's tranquil harbor and seaside locale have been luring painters and other romantic types here for more than 70 years.

◉ Sights & Activities

The 300-mile **Superior Hiking Trail** (www. shta.org) follows the lake-hugging ridgeline between Duluth and the Canadian border. Along the way it passes dramatic red-rock overlooks and the occasional moose and black bear. Trailheads with parking lots pop up every 5 to 10 miles, making it ideal for day hikes. The **Superior Shuttle** (✔218-834-5511; www.superiorhikingshuttle.com; from $20; ☺Fri-Sun mid-May–mid-Oct) makes life even easier, picking up trekkers from 17 stops along the route. Overnight hikers will find 94 backcountry campsites and several lodges to cushion the body come nightfall; the trail website has details. The whole footpath is free, with no reservations or permits required. The trail office (p49) in Two Harbors provides maps and planning assistance.

Split Rock Lighthouse State Park   STATE PARK
See p50.

Sawtooth Outfitters   KAYAKING
(✔218-663-7643; www.sawtoothoutfitters.com; 7213 Hwy 61, Tofte; ☺8am-6pm daily May-late Oct & mid-late Dec, 8am-6pm Thu-Mon Jan-early Apr) Offers guided kayaking tours (half-/full day $65/120) for all levels of paddling on the Temperance River and out on Lake Superior, as well as easier jaunts on wildlife-rich inland lakes. Sawtooth also rents mountain bikes (from $24 per day) to pedal over the many trails in the area, including the popular **Gitchi Gami State Bike Trail** (www.ggta.org).

🛏 Sleeping & Eating

★**Hungry Hippie Farm & Hostel**   HOSTEL **$**
(✔218-387-2256;   www.hungryhippiehostel.com; 410 County Rd 14; dm/r $35/69; P✳🛜) If you've ever dreamt of escaping and just getting away from it all, this remote farmhouse-hostel, 8 miles east of Grand Marais, is the place to indulge those fantasies. The rooms are farmhouse chic, straight out of a design magazine. The welcome is warm. Choose from a bunk in a six-bed dorm or your own private room.

★**Northern Rail Traincar Inn**   HOTEL **$$**
(✔218-834-0955 877-834-0955; www.northernrail.net; 1730 Hwy 3; r/ste $159/209; ✳🛜) It doesn't get much cooler than 17 rooms built into renovated train boxcars. Rooms are on the small side, but are quaintly furnished by theme (Victorian, golf, moose, safari). They have private bathrooms and TVs with DVD players. Wi-fi is hit or miss in the steel cars, but it's available in the lobby. Continental breakfast is included.

★**Gun Flint Tavern**   AMERICAN **$$**
(✔218-387-1563; www.gunflinttavern.com; 111 W Wisconsin St; mains $18-25; ☺11am-10pm; 🛜) You'll find excellent soups and sandwiches, the town's best burgers, and an array of heartier evening meals, such as steaks and walleye, at this central restaurant and tavern. A good range of seasonal and popular microbrews pour from the taps, and the adjacent Raven lounge carries on after the restaurant closes. Book in advance for dinner.

ROAD TRIP ESSENTIALS

USA Driving Guide

With a network of interstate highways, enthusiastic car culture and jaw-dropping scenery, the USA is an ideal road-tripping destination, even year-round in some spots.

DRIVER'S LICENSE & DOCUMENTS

All US drivers must carry a valid driving license from their home state, proof of vehicle insurance and their vehicle's registration papers or a copy of their vehicle-rental contract.

Foreign drivers can legally drive in the USA for 12 months using their home driver's license. An International Driving Permit (IDP) isn't required, but will have more credibility with traffic police and will simplify the car-rental process, especially if your home license isn't written in English and/or doesn't have a photo. International automobile associations issue IDPs, valid for one year, for a fee. Always carry your home license with your IDP.

To ride a motorcycle in the USA, you will need either a valid US state motorcycle license or an IDP specially endorsed for motorcycles.

The American Automobile Association (AAA) has reciprocal agreements with some international auto clubs (eg Canada's CAA and AA in the UK). Bring your membership card from home.

INSURANCE

Don't put the key into the ignition if you don't have insurance, which is legally required.

Liability All drivers are required to obtain a minimum amount of liability insurance that

Driving Fast Facts

➡ **Right or left?** Drive on the right.

➡ **Legal driving age** 16

➡ **Top speed limit** 80mph on some highways.

➡ **Best bumper sticker** 'Where the heck is Wall Drug?'

➡ **Best radio station** National Public Radio (NPR)

would cover the damage you might cause to other people and property in case of an accident. Liability insurance can be purchased from rental-car companies for around $18 per day.

Collision For damage to the rental vehicle, a collision damage waiver (CDW) or loss damage waiver (LDW) is available from the rental company for about $30 a day.

Alternative sources Your personal auto insurance may extend to rental cars, so it's worth investigating before purchasing liability or collision from the rental company. Additionally, some credit cards offer reimbursement coverage for collision damages if you rent the car with that credit card; again, check before departing. Most credit-card coverage isn't valid for rentals of more than 15 days or for exotic models, large vans or 4WD Jeeps.

Road Trip Websites

AUTO CLUBS

American Automobile Association (www.aaa.com) Roadside assistance, travel discounts, trip planning and maps for members.

Better World Club (www.betterworldclub.com) Ecofriendly alternative to AAA.

MAPS

America's Byways (www.fhwa.dot.gov/byways) Inspiring itineraries, maps and directions for scenic drives.

Google Maps (http://maps.google.com) Turn-by-turn driving directions with estimated traffic delays.

Waze (www.waze.com) Popular, free crowdsourced traffic and navigation app.

GasBuddy (www.gasbuddy.com) Website and app that finds the cheapest places to gas up nearby.

ROAD CONDITIONS & CLOSURES

US Department of Transportation (www.fhwa.dot.gov/trafficinfo) Links to state and local road conditions, traffic and weather.

RENTING A VEHICLE

Most rental companies require that you have a major credit card, be at least 25 years old and have a valid driver's license.

Cars

Rental car rates generally include unlimited mileage, but expect surcharges for additional drivers and one-way rentals. Airport locations may have cheaper base rates but higher add-on fees. If you get a fly-drive package, local taxes may be extra when you pick up the car. Child and infant safety seats are legally required; reserve them (around $14 per day) when booking your car.

Some major national companies offer 'green' fleets of hybrid or electric rental cars (eg Toyota Prius or Nissan Leafs), though you'll usually have to pay quite a bit more and reserve far in advance. Many companies rent vans with wheelchair lifts and hand-controlled vehicles at no extra cost, but you must also reserve these well in advance.

The main car-rental companies with branches nationwide:

Alamo (www.alamo.com)

Avis (www.avis.com)

Budget (www.budget.com)

Dollar (www.dollar.com)

Enterprise (www.enterprise.com)

Hertz (www.hertz.com)

National (www.nationalcar.com)

Thrifty (www.thrifty.com)

Other options:

Car Rental Express (www.carrentalexpress.com) Search for independent car-rental companies, specialty cars (eg hybrids) and companies that rent to young drivers (age 18 to 24).

Wheelchair Getaways (www.accessiblevans.com) Rents wheelchair-accessible vans across the country.

Zipcar (www.zipcar.com) Car-sharing club in dozens of cities; some foreign drivers are eligible for membership.

If you don't mind no-cancellation policies or which company you rent from, you may find better deals on car rentals through online travel discounters such as **Priceline** (www.priceline.com) and **Hotwire** (www.hotwire.com).

Motorcycles

Motorcycle rentals and insurance are very expensive, with steep surcharges for one-way rentals. Try these:

Eagle Rider (www.eaglerider.com) Motorcycle rentals and tours in major cities nationwide.

Harley-Davidson (www.harley-davidson.com) Links to scores of local motorcycle shops that rent Harleys.

RVs & Campervans

Popular with road-trippers, recreational vehicles (RVs, also called motorhomes) are cumbersome to drive and burn fuel at an alarming rate. They do solve transportation, accommodation and self-catering kitchen needs in one fell swoop. Even so, there are many places in national parks and scenic areas (eg narrow mountain roads) that they can't be driven.

Make reservations for RVs and smaller campervans as far in advance as possible. Rental costs vary by size and model; basic rates often don't include mileage, bedding or kitchen kits, vehicle prep and cleaning or additional taxes and fees. If bringing pets is allowed, a surcharge may apply.

National rental agencies:

Cruise America (www.cruiseamerica.com) Has 127 RV rental locations.

El Monte RV (www.elmonterv.com) RV rentals in several states.

Jucy Rentals (www.jucyusa.com) Campervan rentals in Los Angeles, San Francisco and Las Vegas.

USA RV Rentals (www.usarvrentals.com) Rentals in major cities coast to coast.

BRINGING YOUR OWN VEHICLE

Citizens of Canada and Mexico who are driving across the border should be sure to bring their vehicle's registration papers, proof of liability insurance valid for driving in the USA and their home driving license. An International Driving Permit (IDP) isn't required, but may be helpful. Only some rental-car companies allow their vehicles to be driven across international borders.

MAPS

Tourist information offices and visitor centers distribute free but often very basic maps. GPS navigation can't be relied upon everywhere, notably in thick forests and remote mountain, desert and canyon areas. If you're planning on doing a lot of driving, you may want a more detailed fold-out road map or map atlas, such as those published by **Rand McNally** (www.randmcnally.com). Members of the American Automobile Association (AAA) and its international auto-club affiliates (bring your membership card from home) can pick up free maps at AAA branch offices nationwide.

Driving Problem-Buster

What should I do if my car breaks down? Put on your hazard lights (flashers) and carefully pull over to the side of the road. Call the roadside emergency assistance number for your auto club or rental-car company. Otherwise, call information (411) for the number of the nearest towing service or auto-repair shop.

What if I have an accident? If you're safely able to do so, move your vehicle out of traffic and onto the road's shoulder. For minor collisions with no major property damage or bodily injuries, be sure to exchange driver's license and auto-insurance information with the other driver, then file a report with your insurance provider or notify your car-rental company as soon as possible. For major accidents, call 911 and wait for the police and emergency services to arrive.

What should I do if I'm stopped by the police? Don't get out of the car unless asked. Keep your hands where the officer can see them (ie on the steering wheel). Always be courteous. Most fines for traffic or parking violations can be handled by mail or online within a 30-day period.

What happens if my car gets towed? Call the local non-emergency police number and ask where to pick up your car. Towing and vehicle storage fees accumulate quickly, up to hundreds of dollars for just a few hours or a day, so act promptly.

Drunk Driving

The maximum legal blood-alcohol concentration for drivers is 0.08%. Penalties for 'DUI' (driving under the influence of alcohol and/or drugs) are severe, including heavy fines, driver's license suspension, court appearances and/or jail time. Police may give roadside sobriety checks to assess if you've been drinking or using drugs. If you fail, they'll require you to take a breath, urine or blood test to determine the level of drugs and alcohol in your body. Refusing to be tested is treated the same as if you'd taken the test and failed.

ROAD CONDITIONS

The USA's highways are not always perfect ribbons of unblemished asphalt. Common road hazards include potholes, rockfalls, flooding, fog, wandering wildlife, commuter traffic jams on weekday mornings and afternoons, and drivers distracted by technology, kids and pets or blinded by road rage.

In places where winter driving is an issue, many cars are fitted with steel-studded snow tires, while snow chains can sometimes be required in mountain areas. Driving off-road, or on dirt roads, is often forbidden by car-rental companies, and it can be very dangerous in wet weather.

Major highways, expressways and bridges in some urban areas require paying tolls. Sometimes tolls can be paid using cash (bills or coins), but occasionally an electronic toll-payment sensor is required. If you don't have one, your vehicle's license plate will likely be photographed and you'll be billed later, usually at a higher rate. Ask about this when picking up your rental vehicle to avoid surprising surcharges on your final bill after you've returned the car.

ROAD RULES

➡ Drive on the right-hand side of the road.

➡ Talking or texting on a cell (mobile) phone while driving is illegal in most states.

➡ The use of seat belts is required in every state except New Hampshire, and child safety seats or seat belts for children under 18 years are required in every state.

➡ In some states, motorcyclists are required to wear helmets.

➡ High-occupancy vehicle (HOV) lanes marked with a diamond symbol are reserved for cars with multiple occupants, but sometimes only during specific signposted hours.

➡ On interstate highways, the speed limit is usually 70mph (though it's higher in a handful of states). Unless otherwise posted, the speed limit is generally 55mph or 65mph on state highways, 25mph to 35mph in cities and towns and as low as 15mph in school zones. It's illegal to pass a school bus when its lights are flashing.

➡ Unless signs prohibit it, you may turn right at a red light after first coming to a full stop – note that turning right on red is illegal in NYC.

➡ At four-way stop signs, cars should proceed in order of arrival; when two cars arrive simultaneously, the one on the right has the right of way. When in doubt, just politely wave the other driver ahead.

➡ When emergency vehicles (ie police, fire or ambulance) approach from either direction, carefully pull over to the side of the road.

➡ In many states, it's illegal to carry 'open containers' of alcohol in a vehicle, even if they're empty.

➡ Most states have strict anti-littering laws; throwing trash from a vehicle may incur a $1000 fine.

PARKING

Free parking is plentiful in small towns and rural areas, but scarce and often expensive in cities. Municipal parking meters and centralized pay stations usually accept coins and credit or debit cards. Parking at broken meters is often prohibited; where allowed, the posted time limit still applies.

When parking on the street, carefully read all posted regulations and restrictions (eg 30-minute maximum, no parking during scheduled street-cleaning hours) and avoid colored curbs, or you may be ticketed and towed. In many towns and cities, overnight street parking is prohibited downtown and in designated areas reserved for local residents with permits.

At city parking garages and lots, expect to pay at least $2 per hour and $10 to $45 for all-day or overnight parking. For valet parking at hotels, restaurants, nightclubs etc, a flat fee of $5 to $40 is typically charged. Tip the valet attendant $2 to $5 when your keys are handed back to you.

FUEL

Many gas stations in the USA have fuel pumps with automated credit-card pay screens. Some machines ask for your zip code after you swipe your card. For foreign travelers, or those with cards issued outside the US, you'll have to pay inside before fueling up. Just indicate how much you'd like to put on the card. If there's still credit left over after you fuel up, pop back inside and the attendant will put the difference back on your card.

SAFETY

Vehicle theft, break-ins and vandalism are a problem mostly in urban areas. Be sure to lock your vehicle's doors, leave the windows rolled up and use any anti-theft devices that have been installed (eg car alarm, steering-wheel lock). Do not leave any valuables visible inside your vehicle; instead, stow them in the trunk before arriving at your destination, or else take them with you once you've parked.

Road Distances (miles)

	Atlanta	Boston	Chicago	Dallas	Denver	El Paso	Houston	Las Vegas	Los Angeles	Miami	New Orleans	New York	Oklahoma City	Phoenix	Portland	Salt Lake City	San Francisco	Seattle	St Louis
Boston	1100																		
Chicago	720	1005																	
Dallas	790	1770	935																
Denver	1405	2005	1010	785															
El Paso	1425	2405	1490	635	700														
Houston	800	1860	1090	240	1030	750													
Las Vegas	1990	2755	1760	1225	750	725	1475												
Los Angeles	2210	3025	2035	1445	1025	815	1560	275											
Miami	660	1510	1380	1320	2070	1940	1190	2545	2750										
New Orleans	475	1530	930	525	1305	1100	350	1740	1915	860									
New York	870	215	800	1565	1800	2200	1655	2550	2820	1290	1310								
Oklahoma City	865	1690	790	210	675	695	450	1125	1345	1500	725	1470							
Phoenix	1860	2690	1800	1070	825	430	1185	285	375	2370	1535	2480	1010						
Portland	2605	3120	2130	2030	1260	1630	2270	1020	965	3265	2555	2925	1925	1335					
Salt Lake City	1880	2395	1405	1265	535	865	1505	420	690	2545	1785	2190	1205	655	765				
San Francisco	2510	3100	2145	1750	1270	1190	1940	570	380	3130	2295	2930	1645	750	635	745			
Seattle	2675	3070	2065	2105	1330	1725	2345	1165	1150	3335	2630	2865	2000	1490	175	840	810		
St Louis	555	1190	295	630	855	1195	840	1615	1840	1215	680	955	500	1505	2050	1325	2065	2120	
Washington DC	635	440	700	1330	1690	1965	1415	2460	2690	1055	1090	230	1345	2350	2820	2095	2835	2770	845

USA Travel Guide

GETTING THERE & AWAY

Every visitor entering the USA from abroad needs a passport. Visitors from most countries only require a passport valid for their intended period of stay in the USA. However, nationals of certain countries require a passport valid for at least six months longer than their intended stay. For a country-by-country list, see the latest 'Six-Month Club Update' from US Customs and Border Protection (www.cbp.gov).

If your passport does not meet current US standards, you'll be turned back at the border. All visitors wishing to enter the USA under the Visa Waiver Program must have an e-Passport with a digital photo and an integrated RFID chip containing biometric data.

For more information on visa requirements, see 'Visas' in the Directory.

AIR

Major international gateway and domestic hub airports across the USA include:

Atlanta Hartsfield-Jackson International Airport (ATL; www.atl.com)

Boston Logan International Airport (BOS; www.massport.com/logan-airport)

Chicago O'Hare International Airport (ORD; www.flychicago.com)

Dallas/Fort Worth International Airport (DFW; www.dfwairport.com)

Denver International Airport (DEN; www.flydenver.com)

Houston George Bush Intercontinental Airport (IAH; www.fly2houston.com)

Las Vegas McCarran International Airport (LAS; www.mccarran.com)

Los Angeles International Airport (LAX; www.flylax.com)

Miami International Airport (MIA; www.miami-airport.com)

Newark Liberty International Airport (EWR; www.panynj.gov/airports)

New York John F Kennedy International Airport (JFK; www.panynj.gov/airports)

Phoenix Sky Harbor International Airport (PHX; www.skyharbor.com)

San Francisco International Airport (SFO; www.flysfo.com)

Seattle-Tacoma International Airport (SEA; www.portseattle.org/Sea-Tac)

Washington Dulles International Airport (IAD; www.metwashairports.com) Near Washington, DC.

If you are flying to the US, the first airport that you land in is where you must go through immigration and customs, even if you're flying to another destination. Upon arrival, all international visitors must register with the Department of Homeland Security, which involves having your fingerprints scanned and a digital photo taken.

Most midsized and larger US airports have car-rental counters staffed by major international agencies in the arrivals area near baggage claim. Courtesy shuttles usually wait curbside to transport rental-car customers to each company's on- or off-site parking lot.

Always make airport car-rental reservations in advance to ensure a car is available, as well as to lock in the lowest rental rates and minimize wait times.

CAR & MOTORCYCLE

On weekends and holidays, especially during summer, traffic at the main border crossings between the USA and its neighboring countries Canada and Mexico can be heavy and waits long. Check current border-crossing wait times online with **US Customs & Border Protection** (https://bwt.cbp.gov).

Be sure to bring all necessary documentation with you, including your vehicle's registration papers, proof of liability insurance and your home driver's license. Occasionally law-enforcement and customs authorities from the USA, Canada or Mexico will decide to search a car very thoroughly for contraband or undeclared dutiable items.

TRAIN

For Canadians living near the US border, taking the train can be an economical option. It also eliminates the hassle of driving a car across the border, which some rental companies do not allow. Instead, you can just rent a car upon arrival in the USA, then return it before leaving.

The USA's national passenger railway, **Amtrak** (www.amtrak.com), operates cross-border trains, including to and from Toronto, ON; Montréal, QC; and Vancouver, BC. Immigration and customs inspections at the US–Canada border can delay trains by an unpredictable amount of time.

Rental car pick-ups are available at some bigger Amtrak train stations in the USA, but usually only with advance bookings. Expect your choice of rental-car companies to be more limited than at airports.

DIRECTORY A–Z

ACCOMMODATIONS

Budget-conscious options for road-trippers include campgrounds, hostels and motels. Motels are ubiquitous on both highways and byways, while hostels are only common in cities and some popular vacation destinations. A variety of camping options exist, from free, bare-bones wilderness tent sites to full-service RV parks with wi-fi and swimming pools.

At midrange motels and hotels, expect clean, decently sized rooms with a private bathroom, cable TV, wi-fi, air-conditioning and perhaps a minibar, microwave and writing desk. If it's included, breakfast might be just fruit, pastries and coffee, or a

Plan Your Stay Online

For more accommodations reviews by Lonely Planet authors, check out http://hotels.lonelyplanet.com. You'll find independent reviews, as well as recommendations on the best places to stay.

full hot-and-cold breakfast buffet. A shared internet computer for guests to use may be available, usually in the lobby.

Top-end hotels and luxury resorts offer many more amenities (eg swimming pool, fitness room, business center, restaurants and bars) and sometimes a scenic location or edgy contemporary design. Additional parking, internet and 'resort' fees may add $10 to $50 or more per day.

B&Bs are smaller and more homey than other accommodation types. Many are high-end romantic retreats in restored historic homes that are run by personable, independent innkeepers who serve gourmet breakfasts. European-style B&Bs also exist: these may be rooms in someone's home, with plainer furnishings, simpler breakfasts, shared bathrooms and cheaper rates. B&Bs can close out of season, and many do not allow children or pets. Reservations are essential.

Rates & Reservations

Rates peak in high season (June to August for summer resort areas, January to February for ski destinations). Generally, mid-week rates are lower, except at business-oriented hotels in cities, where weekend rates may be cheaper.

For all but the cheapest places and the slowest seasons, reservations are advised. In tourist hot spots, book accommodations at least three months ahead in high season – or up to a year ahead in popular national parks such as the Grand Canyon, Yosemite and Yellowstone.

Many hotels offer specials on their websites, while low-end chains sometimes give a slightly better rate over the phone. Chain hotels also offer frequent-flier mileage deals and other rewards programs; ask when booking.

If you plan to arrive late in the evening, you may want to call ahead on the day of your stay to ask the front desk to hold your room. Hotels commonly overbook, but if you've guaranteed your reservation with a credit card, they should accommodate you regardless.

Even if motels or hotels advertise that 'children sleep free,' this may be true only if kids use existing bedding in their parents' room. Requesting a rollaway bed or cot may cost extra.

Helpful Resources

➡ B&Bs
Sites with listings include www.bbonline.com and www.bnbfinder.com.

➡ Camping
KOA (www.koa.com) Private RV parks and campgrounds.

Recreation.gov (www.recreation.gov) For national parks.

ReserveAmerica (www.reserveamerica.com) For state parks.

➡ Hostels
Hostelling International USA (www.hiusa.org) Operates some 50 hostels in the USA.

Hostelworld (www.hostelworld.com) and **Hostelz** (www.hostelz.com) For properties not affiliated with HI-USA.

➡ Hotels & Motels
Discount booking sites include **Hotels.com**, **Hotwire** (www.hotwire.com) and **Booking.com**. **Hotel Tonight** (www.hoteltonight.com) offers fewer properties, but higher quality ones.

➡ House & Apartment rentals
Main booking sites are **Airbnb** (www.airbnb.com) and **Vrbo** (www.vrbo.com).

Sleeping Price Ranges

In this book, the following price ranges refer to a double room in high season, excluding taxes (which can add 10% to 15%).

$ less than $150

$$ $150–$250

$$$ more than $250

ELECTRICITY

Type A
120V/60Hz

Type B
120V/60Hz

FOOD

At most restaurants, lunch is more casual, generally cheaper and sometimes half the price of dinner. Some diners and cafes serve breakfast all day, and a few stay open 24 hours. Weekend brunch is typically available from mid-morning until early afternoon on Saturdays and Sundays.

Dress codes rarely apply except at top-end restaurants, where a collared shirt and possibly a jacket may be required for men. More often than not, smoking is illegal indoors at restaurants; ask first or look around for an ashtray before lighting up on an outdoor patio or at sidewalk tables. Don't expect your neighbors to be happy about inhaling secondhand smoke.

You can bring your own wine (BYOB) at many restaurants, although a 'corkage' fee of $10 to $30 may be charged. If two diners share one main course, there's sometimes a split-plate surcharge. Vegetarians and travelers with food allergies or other dietary restrictions can usually be accommodated, especially in urban areas and at popular vacation destinations.

It's perfectly fine to bring kids along to casual restaurants, where high chairs, booster seats, special kids' menus, crayons and paper placemats for drawing are often available. Look for the family-friendly icon included with listings throughout this book.

LGBTIQ+ TRAVELERS

Most major US cities have a visible and open LGBTIQ+ community that is easy to connect with. Same-sex marriage was legalized nationwide by the US Supreme Court in 2015, and a 2019 Pew Research survey showed a majority of Americans (61%) support same-sex marriage.

The level of acceptance varies nationwide. In some places, there is absolutely no tolerance whatsoever, and in others acceptance is predicated on LGBTIQ+ people not 'flaunting' their sexual preference or identity. Bigotry still exists. In rural areas and conservative enclaves, it's unwise to be openly out, as violence and verbal abuse can sometimes occur. When in doubt, assume locals follow a 'don't ask, don't tell' policy.

Helpful Resources

The Queerest Places: A Guide to Gay and Lesbian Historic Sites, by Paula Martinac, is full of juicy details and history, and covers the country. Visit her blog at www.queerestplaces.com.

Practicalities

Smoking The majority of states prohibit smoking inside all public buildings, including airports, hotels, restaurants and bars.

Time The continental USA has four time zones: Eastern (GMT/UTC -5), Central (GMT/UTC -6), Mountain (GMT/UTC -7) and Pacific (GMT/UTC -8). Daylight saving time (DST), when clocks are set one hour ahead (except in Arizona and Hawaii), applies from the second Sunday in March to the first Sunday in November.

Radio & TV National Public Radio (NPR) can be found at the lower end of the FM dial. The main TV broadcasting channels are ABC, CBS, NBC, FOX and PBS (public broadcasting); the major cable channels are CNN (news), ESPN (sports), HBO (movies) and the Weather Channel.

Weights & Measures Weights are measured in ounces (oz), pounds (lb) and tons; liquids in fluid ounces (fl oz), pints (pt), quarts (qt) and gallons (gal); and distance in feet (ft), yards (yd) and miles (mi).

Advocate (www.advocate.com) Gay-oriented news website reports on business, politics, arts, entertainment and travel.

Damron (www.damron.com) Publishes the classic gay travel guides, but they're advertiser-driven and sometimes outdated.

LGBT National Help Center (www.glnh.org) Counseling, information and referrals.

Gay Travel (www.gaytravel.com) Online guides to dozens of US destinations.

National LGBTQ Task Force (www.thetaskforce.org) National activist group's website covers news, politics and current issues.

Out Traveler (www.outtraveler.com) Gay-oriented travel articles.

Purple Roofs (www.purpleroofs.com) Lists gay-owned and gay-friendly B&Bs and hotels.

HEALTH

Medical treatment in the USA is high-caliber, but the expense could kill you. Many health-care professionals demand payment at the time of service, especially from out-of-towners and international tourists.

Except for medical emergencies (in which case call 911 or go to the nearest 24-hour hospital emergency room, or ER), phone around to find an urgent-care or walk-in clinic or doctor's office that will accept your insurance.

Keep all receipts and documentation for billing and insurance claims, and later reimbursement. Some health-insurance (eg HMOs) and travel-insurance policies with medical benefits require you to get pre-authorization for treatment over the phone before seeking help.

Pharmacies are abundantly supplied, but you may find that some medications available over the counter in your home country will require a prescription in the USA, and without US health insurance, prescriptions can be shockingly expensive. Bring a signed, dated letter from your doctor describing all medications (including their generic names) that you regularly take.

INTERNET ACCESS

Travelers will have few problems staying connected in the tech-savvy USA. Most hotels, guesthouses, hostels and motels have wi-fi (usually free, though luxury hotels are more likely to charge for access); ask when reserving.

Across the US, most cafes offer free wi-fi. Some cities have wi-fi-connected parks and plazas. If you're not packing a laptop or other web-accessible device, try the public library – most have public terminals (though they have time limits) in addition to wi-fi. Occasionally out-of-state residents are charged a small fee.

If you're not from the US, remember that you will need an AC adapter for your laptop, plus a plug adapter for US sockets; both are available at larger electronics shops, such as Best Buy.

MONEY

Prices in this book are quoted in US dollars and exclude state and local taxes, unless otherwise noted.

ATMs

ATMs are available 24/7 at most banks, and in shopping centers, airports, grocery stores and convenience shops. Most ATMs charge a service fee of $2.50 or more per transaction and your home bank may impose additional charges. Withdrawing cash from an ATM using a credit card usually incurs a hefty fee.

For foreign visitors, ask your bank or credit-card company for exact information about using its cards in stateside ATMs. If you will be relying on ATMs (not a bad strategy), bring more than one card and carry them separately. The exchange rate on ATM transactions is usually as good as you'll get anywhere.

Credit Cards

Major credit cards are almost universally accepted. In fact, it's almost impossible to rent a car or make hotel reservations without one. It's highly recommended that you carry at least one credit card, if only for emergencies. Visa and MasterCard are the most widely accepted.

Foreign visitors may have to go inside to prepay at gas stations, since most pay-at-the-pump options require a card with a US

Tipping Guide

Tipping is *not* optional; only withhold tips in cases of outrageously bad service.

➡ **Airport & hotel porters** $2 per bag, minimum per cart $5

➡ **Bartenders** 15% to 20% per round, minimum per drink $1

➡ **Hotel housekeepers** $2 to $5 per night, left under the card provided

➡ **Restaurant servers** 15% to 20%, unless a gratuity is already charged on the bill

➡ **Taxi drivers** 10% to 15%, rounded up to the next dollar

➡ **Valet parking attendants** At least $2 on return of the keys

zip code. Note, too, that you may be asked to 'sign' for credit card purchases, or face a confused clerk or waiter when your card does not require a signature, as US credit-card companies have yet to embrace the chip-and-PIN method available elsewhere in the world. It's normal for restaurant servers to take your card to a pay station to process instead of allowing you to pay at the table. Mobile pay options (Apple Pay, Google Pay) are becoming increasingly common and are a good way to bridge the technology gap.

> ### Eating Price Ranges
>
> The following price ranges refer to a main course. Tax (5% to 10%) and tip (generally 15% to 20%) is not included in price listings unless otherwise indicated.
>
> **$** less than $15
>
> **$$** $15–25
>
> **$$$** more than $25

OPENING HOURS

Typical opening times are as follows:

Banks 8:30am–4:30pm Monday to Thursday, to 5:30pm Friday (and possibly 9am–noon Saturday)

Bars 5pm–midnight Sunday to Thursday, to 2am Friday and Saturday

Nightclubs 10pm–4am Thursday to Saturday

Post offices 9am–5pm Monday to Friday

Shopping malls 9am–9pm

Stores 9am–6pm Monday to Saturday, noon–5pm Sunday

Supermarkets 8am–8pm, some open 24 hours

PUBLIC HOLIDAYS

On the following national public holidays, banks, schools and government offices (including post offices) are closed, and transportation, museums and other services operate on a Sunday schedule. Holidays falling on a weekend are usually observed the following Monday.

New Year's Day January 1

Martin Luther King Jr Day Third Monday in January

Presidents' Day Third Monday in February

Memorial Day Last Monday in May

Independence Day July 4

Labor Day First Monday in September

Columbus Day Second Monday in October

Veterans' Day November 11

Thanksgiving Fourth Thursday in November

Christmas Day December 25

During spring break, high school and college students get a week off from school so they can overrun beach towns and resorts. This occurs throughout March and April. For students of all ages, summer vacation runs from June to August.

SAFE TRAVEL

Despite its seemingly apocalyptic list of dangers – violent crime, riots, earthquakes, tornadoes, hurricanes, wildfires – the USA is a reasonably safe place to visit. The greatest danger to visitors is traffic accidents (buckle up – it's the law).

For travelers, petty theft is the biggest concern, not violent crime. When possible, withdraw money from ATMs during the day or in well-lit, busy areas at night. When driving, secure valuables in the trunk of your car before arriving at your destination and don't leave valuables in your car overnight. Many hotels provide in-room wall safes, some of which can fit a tablet or laptop computer.

TELEPHONE

Cell Phones

Tri- or quad-band phones brought from overseas will generally work in the USA. However, you should check with your service provider to see if roaming charges apply, as these will turn even local US calls into pricey international calls.

It's often cheaper to buy a compatible prepaid SIM card for the USA, such as those sold by AT&T, which you can insert into your international cell phone to get a local phone number and voicemail. Telestial (www.telestial.com) offers these services.

If you don't have a compatible phone, you can buy inexpensive, no-contract (prepaid) phones with a local number and a set number of minutes, which can be topped up at will. Virgin Mobile, T-Mobile, AT&T and other providers offer phones starting around $20, with a package of minutes starting around $20 for 400 minutes, or $30 monthly for unlimited minutes. Electronics stores such as Radio Shack and Best Buy sell these phones.

Huge swaths of rural America, including many national parks and recreation areas, don't pick up a signal. Check your provider's coverage map.

Dialing Codes

All phone numbers within the USA consist of a three-digit area code followed by a seven-digit local number.

Typically, if you are calling a number within the same area code, you only have to dial the seven-digit number (though if it doesn't work, try adding 1 + the area code at the beginning). If you're calling long distance, dial 1 plus the area code plus the phone number. More information on dialing:

➡ **Emergency (police, fire, ambulance)** ☑ 911

➡ **US country code** ☑1

➡ **Making international calls** ☑011 + country code + area code + local number

➡ **Calling other US area codes or Canada** ☑ 1 + area code + seven-digit local number

➡ **Directory assistance** ☑411 (fee may be charged)

➡ **Toll-free prefix** ☑1-800 (or 888, 877, 866). Some toll-free numbers only work within the US

➡ **Pay-per-call prefix** ☑1-900. These calls are charged at a premium per-minute rate – horoscopes, jokes etc

Phone Cards

If you're traveling without a cell phone or in a region with limited cell service, a prepaid phonecard is an alternative solution. Phonecards typically come precharged with a fixed number of minutes that can be used on any phone, including landlines. You'll generally need to dial an 800 number and enter a PIN (personal identification number) before placing each call. Phonecards are available from online retailers such as amazon.com and at some convenience stores. Be sure to read the fine print, as many cards contain

hidden charges such as 'activation fees' or per-call 'connection fees' in addition to the per-minute rates.

TOURIST INFORMATION

The **Visit the USA** (www.visittheusa.com) website is jam-packed with itinerary planning ideas, top experiences by state, inspirational videos and other useful info.

Any tourist office worth contacting has a website, where you can download free travel guides. Some local offices maintain daily lists of hotel-room availability, but few offer reservation services. All tourist offices have self-service racks of brochures and discount coupons; some also sell maps and books.

State-run 'welcome centers,' usually placed along interstate highways, tend to have free state road maps, brochures and other travel planning materials. These offices are usually open longer hours, including weekends and holidays.

Many cities have an official convention and visitors bureau (CVB). These sometimes double as tourist bureaus, but since their main focus is drawing the business trade, CVBs can be less useful for independent travelers. These entities tend to list only the businesses that are bureau/chamber members, so not all of the town's hotels and restaurants receive coverage – keep in mind that good, independent options may be missing.

Similarly in prime tourist destinations, some private 'tourist bureaus' are really agents that book hotel rooms and tours on commission. They may offer excellent service and deals, but you'll get what they're selling and nothing else.

TRAVELERS WITH DISABILITIES

If you have a physical disability, the USA can be an accommodating place. The Americans with Disabilities Act (ADA) requires all public buildings, private buildings built after 1993 (including hotels, restaurants, theaters and museums) and public transit to be wheelchair accessible. However, call ahead to confirm what is available. Some local tourist offices publish detailed accessibility guides.

All major airlines, Greyhound buses and Amtrak trains will assist travelers with disabilities; just describe your needs when making reservations at least 48 hours in advance. Service animals (guide dogs) are allowed to accompany passengers, but bring documentation. For hand-controlled car and wheelchair-accessible van rentals, see the USA Driving Guide chapter.

Most cities have taxi companies with at least one accessible van, though you'll have to call ahead. Cities with underground transport have varying levels of facilities such as elevators for passengers needing assistance – DC has the best network (every station has an elevator), while NYC has elevators in roughly a quarter of its stations.

Many national and some state parks and recreation areas have wheelchair-accessible paved, graded-dirt or boardwalk trails. US citizens and permanent residents with permanent disabilities are entitled to a free 'America the Beautiful' access pass. Go online (www.nps.gov/findapark/passes.htm) for details.

A helpful organization that advises USA-bound travelers with disabilities on mobility issues, and promotes the global participation of people with disabilities in international exchange and travel programs, is **Mobility International USA** (www.miusa.org).

VISAS

Warning: All of the following information is highly subject to change. US entry requirements keep evolving as national security regulations change. Double-check visa and passport requirements *before* coming to the USA.

The **US State Department** (www.travel.state.gov) maintains the most comprehensive visa information, providing downloadable forms, lists of US consulates abroad and even visa wait times calculated by country.

Currently under the Visa Waiver Program (VWP), citizens of 38 countries (including most EU countries, Japan, the UK, Australia and New Zealand) may enter the USA without a visa for stays of 90 days or less.

If you are a citizen of a VWP country, you do not need a visa *only if* you have a passport that meets current US standards *and* you have received approval from the Electronic System for Travel Authorization (ESTA) in advance. Register online with the Department of Homeland Security at https://esta.cbp.dhs.gov/esta at least 72 hours before arrival; once travel authorization is approved, your registration is valid for two years. The fee, which is payable online, is $14.

Most Canadian citizens with passports that meet current US standards do not need a visa for short-term visits to the USA. Citizens of Mexico usually need to get a non-immigrant or border-crossing 'laser' visa in advance. For more information see www.cbp.gov/travel/us-citizens/western-hemisphere-travel-initiative.

Citizens of all other countries or whose passports don't meet current US requirements will need to apply for a visitor's visa. Best done in your home country, the process costs a nonrefundable fee (minimum $160), involves a personal interview and can take several weeks, so apply early.

BEHIND THE SCENES

SEND US YOUR FEEDBACK

We love to hear from travelers – your comments help make our books better. We read every word, and we guarantee that your feedback goes straight to the authors. Visit **lonelyplanet. com/contact** to submit your updates and suggestions.

Note: We may edit, reproduce and incorporate your comments in Lonely Planet products such as guidebooks, websites and digital products, so let us know if you don't want your comments reproduced or your name acknowledged. For a copy of our privacy policy visit lonelyplanet.com/legal.

ACKNOWLEDGEMENTS

Climate map data adapted from Peel MC, Finlayson BL & McMahon TA (2007) 'Updated World Map of the Köppen-Geiger Climate Classification', Hydrology and Earth System Sciences, 11, 163344.

Cover photograph: Arch Rock, Mackinac Island, Gavin Beasley/Shutterstock ©

THIS BOOK

This 1st edition of Lonely Planet's *Midwest & the Great Lakes Best Road Trips* guidebook was researched and written by Mark Baker, Ryan ver Berkmoes, Ali Lemer and Karla Zimmerman. This guidebook was produced by the following:

Senior Product Editor Angela Tinson

Product Editor Andrea Dobbin

Senior Cartographer Alison Lyall

Book Designer Clara Monitto

Assisting Editors Melanie Dankel, Paul Harding

Cover Researcher Gwen Cotter

Thanks to Hannah Cartmel

INDEX

Ali Lemer Ali has been a Lonely Planet writer and editor since 2007, and has authored guidebooks and travel articles on Russia, NYC, Los Angeles, Melbourne, Bali, Hawaii, Japan and Scotland. A native New Yorker and naturalized Melburnian, Ali has also lived in Chicago, Prague and the UK, and has traveled extensively around Europe and North America.

Karla Zimmerman Karla lives in Chicago, where she eats donuts, yells at the Cubs, and writes stuff for books, magazines, and websites when she's not doing the first two things. She has contributed to 70-plus LP guidebooks and travel anthologies covering destinations in Europe, Asia, Africa, North America and the Caribbean. To learn more, follow her on Instagram and Twitter (@karlazimmerman).

OUR WRITERS

OUR STORY

A beat-up old car, a few dollars in the pocket and a sense of adventure. In 1972 that's all Tony and Maureen Wheeler needed for the trip of a lifetime – across Europe and Asia overland to Australia. It took several months, and at the end – broke but inspired – they sat at their kitchen table writing and stapling together their first travel guide, *Across Asia on the Cheap*. Within a week they'd sold 1500 copies. Lonely Planet was born.

Today, Lonely Planet has offices in the US, Ireland and China, with a network of more than 2000 contributors in every corner of the globe. We share Tony's belief that 'a great guidebook should do three things: inform, educate and amuse'.

Mark Baker Mark is a freelance travel writer with a penchant for offbeat stories and forgotten places. He's originally from the United States, but now makes his home in the Czech capital, Prague. He writes mainly on Eastern and Central Europe for Lonely Planet as well as other leading travel publishers, but finds real satisfaction in digging up stories in places that are too remote or quirky for the guides. Prior to becoming an author, he worked as a journalist for the *Economist*, Bloomberg News and Radio Free Europe, among others.

Ryan ver Berkmoes Ryan has written more than 110 guidebooks for Lonely Planet. He grew up in Santa Cruz, California, which he left at age 17 for college in the Midwest, where he first discovered snow. All joy of this novelty soon wore off. Since then he has been traveling the world, both for pleasure and for work – which are often indistinguishable. Read more at ryanverberkmoes.com and at @ryanvb.

← MORE WRITERS

Published by Lonely Planet Global Limited
CRN 554153
1st edition – Oct 2022
ISBN 978 1 8386 956 68
© Lonely Planet 2022   Photographs © as indicated 2022
10 9 8 7 6 5 4 3 2 1
Printed in China